Oppressed

Oppressed

Escaping the Web of an Abusive Relationship

ELIZABETH BROWN

First edition 2022

Book design by Publishing Push

ISBN 978-1-80227-320-5 (paperback)
ISBN 978-1-80227-321-2 (ebook)

Published by PublishingPush.com

Typeset using Atomik ePublisher from Easypress Technologies

My small network of friends: they know who they are. Without them, my strength was being destroyed, and they gave me love and support to pick me up and walk forward. They saw the incidences and were a massive help in very dark times. I may have only had a small bundle of friends, but they have felt like an army.

Introduction

I have decided to write from my heart and head to see if I can help people. I am writing my story to relieve my symptoms; writing is a therapy to heal for some people. Heal from what? Well, open your mind to the book, and you might see bits of your life through mine.

I understand it is not easy in life; everyone has lumps and bumps in the road. As I explain my story, you might be sitting there, saying, "That's me she is writing about."

I have removed some graphic details to protect you, and hopefully, I have tried to stop you from having any of my nightmares.

Chapter One

I am just an ordinary person who wants to see if I can help someone else out there. Could I rescue someone? How do you start to write a book and get someone to hear you? How do you see if someone can hear you and listen to your issues? You are not mental, or least of all, you're not weird? I am a person that's been made to think that I am different. I have completed fourteen tests later by specialists on my brain; they just tell you it is not you. It's them!

Well, the 125 train from London just hit me. Damm, I am involved, but how can I escape? Hey, but I am in safe hands. I am surrounded by people who can help me - but can they? That is the question… I was a big believer in people doing the right thing. I have changed as a person. I am a shadow of the person I was. I cannot expect others to know who I am. I hate who I became near the end.

Why does life throw you some curveballs?

One day you are in a pub when a cocky yet charming person approaches you, your heart flutters, you're smiling, then next - boom! Fat Bottom Girls by Queen on the jukebox, tapping your fingers on the glass and having an ok time. I was beginning to enter another world unknown to me. What's wrong with wanting to be romanced and surprised? It sounds mental and sick to me now.

I have this theory that by writing down some of my wasted twenty years plus, I can empty my brain and make more space for more extraordinary things to happen. The trouble is, a person's lips move, and I take a deep gulp and a massive step back. All I see is a person running away from situations. It seems that people cause some lies, and it's others that listen. I do not think I was ever made to be loved, least of all since my grandad died 28 years ago. The only person that did not judge me, he accepted me for all my faults. He was my guiding light that never went out until he died; he is just a flicker now. Does this new person entering my life know this before I have spoken? Does it give clues to hurt me on my back?

So, let's make a start; fingers crossed that you get me.

I met Jesse in a local pub. Having never seen him before, he was sitting with two people. I was in this pub getting a drink with a friend called Debs when a man approached me. This character was cocky and full of himself. I now know this to be a man known as Jesse. His friends at the table were Sharon and Graham, who worked in a nearby prison. Jesse revealed his friendship had been established for years; Sharon was like a sister to him.

Jesse, tubby, charming, knowing every step to take and word to say to me to capture my attention. Jesse had a way of explaining his tragic life that was wholly believable and seemed honest enough. I wondered if this was the start of being part of a fantastic lifestyle. I never thought for a minute that I would end up in a dangerous web. I never thought I would not move out of it. I am attached somehow, line by line, in this web, with no scissors, knives, or fire to sever the ties. I am struggling to move, but can I be strong enough to escape?

Little did I know my life would change forever, not just then, but every day since that day back in May 2001.

As his beers began to flow, his friendship with Graham and Sharon is a bought one. His attention towards me increases; Jesse knows exactly what to say and when to make his moves in my space. I think I liked the attention; it had been a while. Was it just too good to be true, or am I such an idiot? This man pulled me in without me even knowing that I was being sucked in. I seemed happy and enjoying the relationship; I would apologise to ensure things ran smoothly. This was easier, and maybe I didn't view the relationship right. Maybe I was damaged, and it was my mistakes that offended and upset him.

Sharon and Graham are heavy drinkers, both with pint glasses, smoking roll-ups. Rough people with a question mark hanging over them? Do they do drugs and take them to prison? Well, that's another question! However, Graham was ok, but Sharon brought out the worst in the cocky yet charming, self-assured other person. I am convinced that Sharon had a long dog lead attached to Jesse.

For the first and second weeks, we would text and speak frequently.

One day, Jesse took me shopping to the large Tesco's at Peterborough; he walked off, so, left with the shopping trolley, I started to place things in there. They were items for my two girls for school and pack ups also for my cat, Mittens. I was beginning to learn quickly that Jesse was a nightmare on a shopping trip. Jesse did need one of those children's reins taped to his wrists and taped to yours!

There came a loud voice shouting, "Darling! Darling, are these yours? Darling, where are you?"

This voice was the volume of a town crier; no one's head could have turned any quicker to understand who was shouting. Oh, and there he was – Jesse, larger than life.

He was still screaming, "Darling, are these in your size?"

When I looked, they were the most enormous leopard skin pants I'd have ever seen. I didn't know whether to laugh or cry with embarrassment. As Jesse came closer to me, he walked up to the elderly couple in the next aisle and gave them to a woman in at least her 70's. Can you imagine your emotions and laughter if that happened to you? It was so funny, yet cringy-

I remember this incident years later, but as I write this all down, I have had to come back and slot this in as a memory. I sincerely hoped there were more fun times than just this one.

It feels like I am blind drunk at times. How did a bloke from nowhere come into my life and make me feel alive yet also pull a fast one on me? Reflecting back now, this was the start. I understand, years later from my counsellor, that you never get with an abuser because they are awful.

Jesse told my friend Debs and me that he was living with Wendy but didn't love her. However, he failed to tell me this next part - Jesse had played away for six years; his parents were part of this deceit.

I found out much later in this horrible toxic web that this was a key piece of information – that should have been a sign for me.

He did not tell me anything else about himself but dug deep about me: I became his sole focus. Is this where I was stupid and unaware of whom I was opposite? Was I supposed to be impressed by his attention? Am I flattered that Jesse was honest with me for what I now know to have been the only time in the twenty years that followed?

Well over 7200 days of my life is not only just one big fat lie but also stealing my enjoyment and denying me happiness. Why didn't I escape? I am such a fool, easily manipulated, and, most of all, I am lost. I was never good at map reading, so I couldn't find my way home. That is if I knew where home was! I haven't been home for a long time, so when I see it, I will struggle; it will all be new to me.

We started our relationship, and as the days and nights flowed by, Jesse came to see me more and more. But a significant incident happened when Jesse said he had to go on a family holiday with Wendy. This did not sit well with me, so I gave him the cold shoulder or frozen shoulder. Being in the Ministry of Defence, I was surrounded by the Forces, mainly males, but I had never mixed work with pleasure before. There was this lovely person called Martin from work, and I asked if his offer to go out for a drink with him was still open. I spoke with him and said that if the drink invitation were still available, I would love to go.

So, I went out with him after about ten days of Jesse and Wendy's holiday. I had a great couple of dates with Martin; he was so kind and caring but was in love with a woman called Heather. She was older than him, and I guess this scared him. I tried to reassure him that he was a fantastic catch; he just needed to work out what he wanted.

While I began to get on with my life, I had a whole new makeover, cut my hair, changed my clothes. Yes, you have guessed it, City Boy called me from Florida every day. I could not see his lies or storytelling, but one thing was for sure I gave him what I thought was to be a hard time. Something within me felt it was wrong, but all the words from him put together seemed logical. Jesse slept in the same bed as Wendy and made out nothing happened; he did not have a good time at all.

"I couldn't let my family down, could I? They would never let me hear the end of it. I have to be a good boy and do as they say."

I put the phone down because I did not believe him; his comments made me doubt all my feelings and thoughts.

I just did not buy it, but when Jesse came back, I accepted his lies... not knowing my original hunch was correct. Why didn't I stick to my original thoughts? Why could Jesse talk me around so quickly? God, it was starting to get annoying how I did not listen to myself as much as I used to do. I thought I would have known that I was being taken for a ride.

Jesse came over, grovelling and saying how he had had an awful time in Florida; he said it made him realise it was all of me he wanted – kids as well. Jesse had sad puppy dog eyes, watering just enough to make you cave in and be forgiving. When I asked Jesse what he wanted, he said everything, including me - quite literally - obviously what I allowed him to take of me. I felt that I was totally overcome with emotion and, deep within those eyes, he seemed sorry for his actions. Yet that is not the truth, is it?

Years later, I found the photos of that holiday which told me that my original hunch was correct. Pictures of her sat on the loo nude – seriously, poor cow.

So, I believed his lies, deception and portrayal of his version of events in that time frame.

Jesse then snuck his way back into my life as if everything were perfect; well, in his eyes, I guess it was. There was always that seed of doubt for me, but with no concrete evidence, I chose to ignore my thoughts. This was hard for me, those gut feelings that you try to ignore. There was a level of honesty within me, yet a huge fear of speaking out. I have always felt that I have someone on my shoulder talking me out of something, and the other someone talks me into it. It's like I have two sides to me. I cannot explain any of it so far, but I am working out what this means, so I hope I can break it down further.

I arranged to take Jesse to meet my mum and dad. The two worlds to come as one was never going to happen. A classic city boy never too far from a takeaway and a pub to a household in the middle of nowhere. No pub for miles, milk deliverer, and postal worker deliveries by a van, getting in the car to the pub was something alien to him. So, when we pulled onto my parents' property, Jesse had lost his head.

My mum and dad were warm to start with him; however, Mum took him onto their patio.

She said, "As far as you can see, the furthest treeline is the end of our land."

Jesse responded with, "You could kill me, bury me under the patio, and no one would know."

My mum, being her, said, "Darling, don't give me ideas."

I laughed because that totally freaked him out.

It was a scary experience for him; its mum's way of putting him in his place on reflection. I think Jesse liked my dad, but I think my mum and dad did not trust him on examination. Not deep down, they didn't. Dad seemed pleased to see me smile and happy - as dads do, I guess.

Chapter Two

As time went by, I would drive from my house to his and back on a weekend. I would cook, iron, be verbally shouted at, and Jesse would throw his weight around. I would clean his house and then go back to mine. I was told I was doing it wrong and that I was useless. I must have been a mug.

One day, I was so tired I nearly crashed the car on the way back to my home with my two small children in the car. Someone that day was looking after me because the driver on the inside lane woke me up. I am sure I had already survived at least 2 of my lives at this stage, but what next would use one of my lives up?

Sharon was a large woman who smoked roll-ups, took drugs, drank pints and got her big, floppy boobs out just to wave you off. Yuk, she was foul-mouthed, bragging about how she could get drugs in and out of her prison. Being in the MOD, I could not be around people doing drugs; it would cost me my job.

When Jesse was around Graham and Sharon, he became a woman-hater, foul-mouthed, loud and bold as brass. So, guess who did not like being in this? I was led to believe these people were his friends – some friends!

One day, Sharon accused me of taking Jesse away from her. She went on to say that she had had the best sex sessions with Jesse possible, and I would never replace her in the bedroom. The penny was dropping.

Jesse started to explain; he and Sharon were like brother and sister. He said I seriously had nothing to worry about. Strange relationship – all too weird for me, and I freaked out. Surrounded by lies, was I to believe her, or for once, was he telling the truth? I reckon I could have started to plant a field full of something all the seeds of doubt. Strange how your mind and distrust emotions work; it's twisted, or is that just how I think?

The following morning, Jesse's dad, Charles, contacted me to ask me some questions about their son Jesse's relationship with Sharon and Graham. I braced myself because Papa was an adorable, quietly spoken person with class. But I was not prepared for what happened; Papa asked if Jesse was doing drugs.

I replied, "No," however, the questions just kept coming.

It all had come to a head because Papa had been out with Sharon's adopted parents for a drink, and they were slagging me off. Let's face it; they thought they had that right. I am a divorcee from twenty-five years ago with two girls. In the Dark Ages, getting with a woman who has two children by another person meant I should have been stoned at a wall. I'm dirty, not good enough for Jesse. Sharon's foster parents had never met me, so instead of meeting and getting to know me, they listened to others. They took at face value what they had heard I was like, via their stepdaughter and flew off on one.

Papa had retaliated by stating that his son wasn't a junkie and he'd got a great girlfriend to keep him in tow. He possibly meant to have said Jesse's speeding tickets were decreasing; I pulled him into line or normal, reasonable behaviour.

For the rest of that night, Jesse went ape, a bit like the old-fashioned pinball machines you used to play in the pubs. You would press the flickers but never know where the ball would go to or bounce from. His temper was something that I had to negotiate to get out of his firing line. Not for the first time, not only could I not contain this argument and calm everyone down, but I also couldn't understand if I had told the truth why he was getting his knickers in such a twist. I guess that was the point I was missing; Jesse didn't believe I was telling the truth.

Jesse was seething out of control; I did my utmost to defend myself and try to prevent a screaming match, get him to be reasonable. At whose expense? I was sobbing, but still, relentlessly, Jesse was verbally charging towards me with gritted teeth, nostrils blowing wide. So, I dashed off from the pub to my home, tail between my legs crying and with 'I haven't done anything wrong,' repeatedly replaying in my mind. Why was I trying to justify or logically balance his enraged outburst when I told nothing but the truth? Papa was so apologetic and friendly to me, too; all I ever meant to do was reassure them that their son wasn't a junkie that I had witnessed. I felt I did the right thing to speak out, but I was beginning to regret saying anything.

Clearly, my mind wasn't in the right place because I went home and downed handfuls of painkillers with some whiskey and lemonade. I remember the first two or three whiskies and lemonades and two painkillers, but from then onwards, it's a total blur.

I woke up in hospital not knowing anything. I didn't have my clothes; they were cut off and thrown on the floor. Pipes and machines sounding, bright lights everywhere. I mumbled to the person nearby and asked what happened; she said I had been found collapsed and brought in. I think I must have been in denial; hours passed where I was so violently sick and feeling grotty. Have I been attacked and smashed over the head with a hammer? My arms were so badly bruised. What's happened to me? How the heck had I got into this place without me knowing about it? I thought I was a controlled person – like, if I got myself in poo street, I would find the exit and would know what to do. I now believe this to be false. Because I am racked with guilt that I didn't do anything or enough. I just sat there waiting to be mistreated. I think I was shutting down; I hid, ducked and dived, avoided stuff, anything to prevent the conflict.

The psychiatrist asked, "What the hell was I thinking of?"

I had no idea who he was, never mind the answer to the question. No sign of Jesse, family, or anything else… What's happened to me? Why am I here?

He said, "Well, young lady, you are a fortunate person whom the person upstairs doesn't want to take just yet."

"Why?"

"Did you know you took enough whiskey and tablets that would have filled a river and killed a lot of fish, never mind all for one person?"

Amazed and confused by his comments, I replied, "Why did I do that?"

The psychiatrist said the person that bought me in dumped me off and then left.

"You were mumbling you had told the truth. You mentioned the noise of the arguments had just got too much for you from what we could make out."

"Oh," I replied.

He stated, "What on earth were you thinking? Have you done this before?"

"Nope."

"So, why now?"

I said, "You've already worked out what's gone on for me to end like this."

"Yes, I have an idea. You love someone so much you would try to kill yourself to prove a point, young lady. I don't ever want to see you in my ward again. Do you hear me? You're different from all the other OD's that come in here. Fix what's wrong and never return, please. You gave us all such a fright."

I worked out for myself that the person who dropped me off was Jesse, the person I was defending - but for what? I did see this sequence of events logically unfold in my eyes and brain. Yet I just needed the truth; then that would be the end of it. But obviously, this wasn't the case at all. How could I get it so wrong? Why am I only viewing it this way?

The psychiatrist gave me a right telling off. Never mind a there, there, softly approach – nope, straight in with a sharp instrument to ram home his views. Funny how in 2021, in the middle of a lockdown pandemic, I can remember word for word what he said to me.

My mum came to see me; it was lovely to see a friendly face, so Jesse had contacted her. My mum took me home, but somehow, I'm not sure to this day; Jesse wormed his way back into my life. Why can't I remember what his following actions were when I can so vividly remember what the psychiatrist had said to me?

Writing all my silly incidents down reminds me why I am doing this. It's a bit like taking information, placing it on a hard drive and removing it to free up some space inside my brain. But most of all, I evidently get to close the lid on it, and it stays on the hard drive. It is pouring out like the Victoria Falls going over the edge of the mountaintop now. I don't see anyone at the top ready to turn the tap off, so I best get cracking on and tell you the rest.

Somehow, Jesse came back into my life.

I had lost significant weight because of my overdose when Chris, my old boss, came to check up on me. He noticed that the belt of my trousers was hanging off my waist. We hugged, which I am sure I was thankful for. I look back now and notice what was happening to me. Why had I let someone raid my head, confuse me, make out I am bonkers? Why did I let them do this much to me? Why was I so weak?

Jesse came round as if nothing had happened, his smug, smiling face a little forced but still smiling. He entered my house with no apology and no discussion, armed with bags and bags of food shopping. This example of behaviour became his apology, no lips saying sorry, but that's the best you get with people like this.

Jesse began lecturing me that he had come round because I needed to look after myself and the girls better. Jesse was creepily friendly - as smooth as chocolate milk. No lumps, just sickly; knowing what words to say and when not to tell them. How does he know what I will respond with before I do? Every step is calculated, all efforts are being monitored for precision to get responses from me. That merry-go-round just keeps going, and I'm on it now with no exit signs and no little person running for the hills. How do I get off? Have I imagined it all?

A shrug of the shoulders and moving on to the following incident without me knowing what was happening. It seems, reflecting on it now,

I was shutting down, ignoring the incidents, closing my eyes and ears to stuff. Why was I doing that? What was wrong with me? I thought I loved life, but what was this, certainly no Cinderella fairy-tale here?

On reflection, it wasn't a life. Sometimes it doesn't matter how long it takes to get out of this; the operative word is "EXIT." "Get out."

Chapter Three

A holiday devised to recuperate was thrown at me last minute; a great part of me wanted it to make this all up to me. However, that devil on my shoulder would be doubting and questioning but without my lips moving. For someone chatty, this isn't normal – say something, do something! Did I hide or lie to myself?

Jesse arranged this holiday with at least ten strangers; Jesse knew three of them and somehow piggybacked their holiday. But this is a calculating person selling me this great holiday! I didn't see the signs, didn't want to.

Over time, I started to piece this together, but the downside was that it took me two decades to see the spider's web that was being built around me.

When we arrived at the airport, I found out we would be flying first-class; wow, wow, wow! What woman wouldn't be blown away? One thing that's always bothered me is why didn't he just explain? Say sorry it was so much cheaper.

I was spinning so fast at this stage, too fast for anyone to get off; I wanted to get off. Eighteen years later, I now feel guilty that I wanted to be loved; I wanted someone to care for me. The trouble is that it cost me nearly two decades to learn the lessons of life of being with the wrong person.

Some people love themselves so much that no one else exists. Jesse was even horrible to animals on several occasions. Jesse was like a bad apple in a basket, infecting everyone with his poison dripping on all the other apples. It just needed someone big and brave to throw that bad apple away to ensure all the other apples didn't become rotten.

The first-class was incredible; how could a woman like me end up in this seat? How could I sit here and think this is where I belong? Pinch me, please! I took all the freebies, napkins with first-class written on them, toothbrush, blankets. I was like a child in an old-fashioned sweet shop. Walking out of the isles onto the tarmac first, I felt like I was someone special walking into that airport. It would be nice later in life to experience it again to understand it's unconditional – no spiders' web.

Arriving in Thailand were memories that should be in your heart forever; it looks like I've buried any happy images. Where are they? Don't I have the key to unlock them? Were they any other images? Why can't I remember? It's so frustrating that I can't remember the good times that got me on this journey in the first place. It's all become one big blur. Have you ever seen a snowball start small and end up the size of a house? Well, just imagine the snowball was the crisis; as it rolled down the hill, it grew by collecting all the loose snow on its way. All the loose snow represents an incident, an issue, a storm.

In Pattaya, we walked with the coach party friends, who suddenly became Jesse's full-time audience. While walking down the street, Jesse was approached by a Thai woman. The cute little Thai woman touched him and pulled him in for kisses; she was stroking his shorts directly on top of his manhood. Not at any point did he tell her to stop, nor did he push her away.

In the sickest of ways, Jesse loved it, laughing loudly to his new friends, saying, "I can't help it if women really want me!"

But is it me again? I was walking down the streets thinking lovely thoughts. Then his hand dropped off mine, and Jesse was lapping it up. Why did I see it this way, everyone around me laughing at it? I found it very disrespectful, and I was angry. I don't feel any remorse in feeling angry anymore about this, yet I can remember it. When it happened to another couple in the group, guess what? Fireworks went off, and she got a taxi straight back to the airport and went home. He spent the rest of the holiday getting bladdered and sleeping around. He didn't go after her!

It was all portrayed that I was overreacting, and I was the issue, yet Nina had a remarkably similar incident and went home. Another argument and another day in paradise... no, but I didn't have the money to get home. I had to wait for him to take me back. I was gutted.

I became sick and spent days and days in the hotel room or sat on the sun lounger, unable to move other than to the bathroom and back. Jesse went drinking, and I got more and more ill. Imagine being in a foreign country, unable to speak the language, not moving for eight days because of crippling sickness and the trots. Your partner, drinking and disappearing more than Shergar. No need to imagine - it was my life, guys. Jesse was nowhere to help, so how could I return home and say the good bits about this venture and trip of a lifetime? I was ashamed of my behaviour which was, I think, not being seen with him. To protect my pride, I learnt how to act and become the boaster he was constantly pushing me to be. I had become someone I didn't recognise anymore; I didn't even know why I was there most of the time. I felt like an accessory picked up and dropped. Yet, in some way, I felt my life was becoming dependable on him. Even if I could get home, he held the passports and money.

Jesse would go to the bars and dominate the singing opportunities. Oh, sorry, let me explain; gosh, I have time to explain what happened! There was a singer in a bar that sang every night, but 'gob almighty' would heckle and shout comments out to her. She eventually gave the mic to him, and over a period, it became they shared the time on stage. This passed into his ego; he would tell me all about him singing and people loving his songs whilst I did the tango to the toilet again. One day he even came into the bathroom to check I was telling the truth about my sickness and illness.

Still to this day, I can hear him in my head. Lecturing me about what a great singer he was but unaware that I didn't want to listen to him being so in love with himself. Why would he? Too selfish to know anything other than himself, I have now decided - too absorbed in himself and that ego of his to care for anyone else.

After hearing about me being so ill, one woman from the group took me to a pharmacy, and she found someone to explain my illness. It wasn't Jesse who took me; it was the coach party woman who had been asking Jesse for days where I was. What had Jesse been telling them? More lies, I reckon, bet he said I was moody. Then he would have had free rein to do what Jesse likes when Jesse likes. Still true to this very day. Jesse does what Jesse wants when Jesse wants; the big I am with the big I am nothing. What Jesse can't take from you, Jesse has ways of grinding you down until you give in.

After getting some treatment, I couldn't wait to get out of there; I still don't know if it was to get away from him or these things: Jesse flirting with the Thai boxer's girlfriend and befriending the owner of an Irish Bar. It all just gave him carte blanche to be louder and louder. A bit like the overdose, I have now made this a picture of a life not worth living or fighting for.

Chapter Four

One day, Jesse stayed over at my place; my two girls were at school during the day, away at most weekends. I was in the local pub; Graham and Sharon were there, loud, threatening and intimidating me at every opportunity. Jesse went to the bar this day to get the next round, and Sharon instructed Graham to help Jesse at the bar with the drinks. She turned to me and continued to rant that she was the best sex Jesse had ever had, and I would always be second-best to her. She was growling with her hairy lip and male-like clothes on, making a point that she had no underwear on again.

When the men came back from the bar, Jesse noticed I wasn't happy. Sharon was acting as if nothing had been said or happened. But I couldn't just sit there and pretend, nor could I tell my face that, so soon after this incident. But it had all been made out that I had issues... Where was the truth when I tried to defend myself...? It all collapsed around me. I thought Jesse said his relationship with Sharon was like the sister he never had.... So that's why they had been sleeping with each other....? Weird: it's not just me, is it?

Jesse hit the roof and, in the middle of this pub, he erupted and accused me of causing an issue between him and his friends. So, I left, and he came back to my house around eight hours later – bladdered.

Jesse was raging, foam just stopping short of his lips, furious, so I knew by this time in my life to learn to duck and dive out-of-the-way of his temper. I was starting to become fearful of his temper and behaviours. I thought Jesse would beat me senseless; he kept repeatedly telling me it was all in my head, that I had imagined it all. This made my head even more messed up - even at this early stage. I did not know what to do to stop it. Who would know I would become an expert at this negotiation? Open University doesn't teach that course; it's one of life's skills I guess I gained.

Jesse often stayed at mine; uninvited, I add, at these early stages, Jesse would dominate when he stayed over and when he didn't.

But the irony of this is that the following day when Jesse came back, he climbed over the bath for the overhead shower, and his back went. Mmmm, I hear you say. He was screaming down the stairs, bellowing as if I were ten streets away. I called the local doctor out, who gave him an injection. There are times now I wished it had been conducted in a particular American State that does this. Then after this method, it all goes quiet.

Jesse later lost all feeling and bodily function below the crushed discs in his back. I took time off work to care for him; it was a pity I didn't have that malicious bone in my body to put something in his drinks. I left him a container to pee into, I washed him, but none of it was ever correct. Funny, his back going stopped his arms working too, also he couldn't feed himself, laid there like a big fat blob demanding this and the other. Like an idiot, I complied with his every request until I returned to work, left sandwiches, pee container right next to him – still wrong, though.

His dad, Charles, a lovely person, gracious and dignified, came to collect Jesse from my house. Jesse went back home to West Midlands to have an operation on his back. I thought they would remove the bad bits, no such luck, but they did repair the crushed discs. This enabled him to be treated in West Midlands and return to his house.

The nurses were screaming for me to take him. "Good luck, Hun; he's been a blooming pain. Ringing the bell, like a toddler."

The staff couldn't wait to see the back of him; this was a beautiful private hospital, lovely staff where you had red wine with your meals.

Getting him in the car was nothing short of a bloody nightmare, screaming in pain, demanding, shouting at me. As I turned the ignition on, more screams let out. Did you know I had deliberately hurt him by just turning the key? I was accused of driving over every pothole to cause him intensive pain! Well, I didn't have that knowledge either.

So, on bringing him back to his house, I got him all comfy, settled, and like everything, the bad penny arrived - his mother. Harsh, you might think, but I'm writing down incidences that happened nearly two decades ago, so I know this to be the truth now. His mother was blooming awful most times, but when you were seriously in trouble, she came into her own. I nicknamed her the 'Smother-in-Law' for many reasons. There was no filter on Smother's mouth. Everything was disconnected from brain to mouth and just fell out. And God help you if you tried to comment on her chit chat. She would totally suffocate and browbeat you down into submission. It came to the point to ignore her and keep your thoughts to yourself. It was easier to pick your battles with her; the force and threats aimed towards you told you this.

As the Smother-in-Law sat near her precious bloody son, I got the 600 denier stockings he needed to have on. Every time I moved his foot, Jesse would scream so loudly it was deafening. I made a cup of tea for his Smother, not that she ever noticed. I had only been dating Jesse for 11 months at this stage. I had become his full-time slave, someone to scream at, someone to manipulate. Someone to bully, drag down, then you lose all your sparkle.

Out of nowhere, his Smother slapped her son's leg and said, "Don't you think my boy is well endowed?"

Taken aback, I slapped his other leg and said, "I've had bigger."

Well, you should have seen her face! The start of my life with the Smother and her son, joining forces to become hell.

I have no idea why I responded so quickly or why I said what I did. I found a mother saying this in front of her 37-year-old only son and his new girlfriend disturbing and very weird. Oh, and by the way, he really wasn't that big! Just saying.

The following morning, I thought everything was fine and dandy; I cleaned the worktops as I had cooked and cleaned each visit. I was fully dressed when I was accused of upsetting Jesse's Smother; I didn't know that I had said anything to worry her. As I tried my best to defend myself and get him to laugh it off, the worse it was for me. I did get angry because I felt unheard, stamped on and misunderstood. It was just a response that came from the hip; I didn't think it through, but let's be honest, it was not worth a full-blown argument. My nerves were playing up to the point that I ended spilling a cup of tea right near him. He retaliated with a full-blown smack across my face.

The handprint was visual to see; it lasted for a couple of days, so I made up an excuse to have a day off work come Monday morning. Because I sounded off, different, not like myself, my boss, Chris, asked me to meet him for a coffee; he must have known. He was kind and loving and asked me to take a couple of days off until the hand mark had disappeared. I was defending Jesse's smack because I had spilt tea; Chris logically balanced me back into perspective again. I felt sick, hurt, physically and mentally drained.

As life went by, my life became one big mess; I was losing my sparkle. I often thought I was a rubbish human being/girlfriend morning dinner and night; it was also hammered into me. Was I so incapable of loving anyone, misunderstanding everything all the time, killing off friend-ships? Was I that evil and calculating? I didn't think I was, but I guess looking back, I was letting that virus in for a moment. You can't then get it out until it's been all-around your body, causing havoc along the way. Are we still talking about Jesse here or the virus…? Not sure.

Jesse's negative attitude left me questioning everything about myself and my abilities to be a parent. A worker. A friend even! What use was I to society when all I could see all the time was everything I did wrong? The constant put-downs, but hey, wait a minute, there must have been some good times.

Well, I suppose I should have been grateful when Jesse offered me his ex-live-in girlfriends' things, saying, "I've bought all her things anyway; I own them." Selling the idea for me to have his girlfriend Wendy's belongings just didn't cut it.

"They are all designer stuff. I brought them all. You don't have anything, anyway; why don't you just take hers?"

20

I was told I was ungrateful; I was a low life from the gutter.

I climbed into his bed, and we barely spoke; Jesse couldn't work out what was wrong with the gifting. It's obviously just me; I'm the ungrateful one. How dare I refuse such gifts? Why am I the one lying here thinking about what I could do to make this right? I did nothing wrong, but clearly, the virus at this point has spread. Jesse is always right, isn't he?

Later that night, the Nokia 3310's mine and his were on charge on my side of our bed. Mmmm, another issue I had never envisaged. One of the Nokia phones received a text just after midnight, half-asleep, half-not; the text said, 'Babes, last night was so sensual, can't wait to see you again.'

Blurred eyed, I looked, read it, and then put it down. Confused and dazed, I went back to the phone, and I continued to reread it. Then the penny from the machines in the arcades finally dropped - "It's not my phone I'm reading. Shoot."

I got up and took the phone downstairs, and I responded to that text. I know, I can hear you screaming - don't do it.

Too late, I text, sorry, I can't remember who you are.

She immediately responded. 'After these months, I thought I meant something to you… Did you read my letter? Love you xx'

Even more confused, I started to search for this letter. Knowing his house was a little untidy, I knew roughly where he placed everything. So, I returned to the main bedroom, where Jesse had no idea what I was doing, sleeping his little head off. I carefully opened the chest of drawers in that room that Jesse constantly screamed at me to stay away from. Why did he? Well, that all became clear.

I found a letter from Angie, who was obviously involved with Jesse; I went downstairs to read it, and Jesse was none the wiser. The letter was beautifully written and dated, declaring her love and Jesse's involvement with her son. Angie made it clear she loved him and couldn't bear to be apart.

So, I went upstairs, turned on the landing light, and the beast awoke. Screaming and swearing at me, I stated what had happened word for word, from the phones to the letter I held in my hand.

Jesse shouted his innocence to me, then rolled over and tried to go back to sleep. "You shouldn't go snooping. Always take it on the chin if you go through my things."

So, let's get this right. Jesse was living with Wendy for six years but knocking Angie and me off, too. Seriously, I was so confused. Was this right? So, let's just get this straight, there was Angie, Wendy and Rani: three others - and they all had left him. Some chose to leave at Christmas, and normal people would be heartbroken. Nope, not this one; he would slag them all off: alcoholics, they're mad, violent. Not once did he draw a breath that six live-in girlfriends all left him… Something tells me that his past was catching up with him. He now has an ex-wife and a child that are not with him too. What a record.

I immediately grabbed my clothes, went into the bathroom, and got ready to leave. Jesse came out of the bedroom and wouldn't let me out of the bathroom, saying accusations and somehow, again, I had this all wrong. I opened the window to see if I could jump down, but I thought I would break something doing it from the first floor. We had been drinking. I'd admit yes, we had. But I hadn't got this wrong! Jesse continued to stop me from leaving; I was hell-bent on getting the heck out of there. Jesse has always had a great way of words, and he talked me around again - as he always did. I sobbed myself to sleep; Jesse held me, saying he would get me some help.

As I awoke, I got out of there as quick as I could. I ran. I know that running at my age is a health and safety issue in itself, but I didn't look back. I did go to the counselling session Jesse had arranged. The strange thing is that he came in with me; looking back, I now know why. I thought it was because Jesse was supportive; I now believe it's a form of control. Eighteen years ago, I didn't hear of Domestic Abuse unless a murder took place by either the wife or husband.

I struggled to understand my actions or involvement, but I took his actions to be a genuine act of kindness. Maybe I did need help? It was clear I felt I was beyond help. Could anyone help me? Thousands of questions and with no answers.

Within the session, the lady had a polite face and a smile. She listened intently to what Jesse was saying about, in his words, the sequence of events. I remember it distinctly not happening that way, but I went along with it. Partly because I was out of it, I can't explain what I mean by that, but that's how I feel and how I felt at the time. I was silent for most of the session, and while his lips were moving, I thought, when will I be able to speak? The counsellor obviously wanted to talk too but couldn't get a word in or a word out of me, which is undoubtedly the point of the session.

The counsellor asked him to leave, and you should have seen the look on his face. Someone had taken the decision from him, and guess what, Jesse was not happy.

I spoke briefly with the counsellor, who was the first person ever to say, "You know Jesse has issues, and not all of this is you, don't you"?

"No, I didn't know; I thought it was all me."

"No, it is not, love."

When I left to get back in his car, I distinctively remember the constant bombardment of questions about what I had been asked and my responses to be quite overpowering.

But nevertheless, in another incident, I thought it was just that Jesse cared for my wellbeing. Some people have a sick note excuse book; I clearly had a book of excuses to deny myself the truth and clarify the correct flow of events. I genuinely thought Jesse was trying to help me. I felt it was a trap, but I denied my thoughts to bin them at the first opportunity.

Chapter Five

To say sorry for the incident in the bathroom, Jesse took me to Worcester for a romantic meal. I thought it was ideal, and he was showing me his sorrow for his actions. I went to the loo because I felt safe to do so; not sure why I say that, but I remember thinking it was all excellent... As I came back, a charming waitress was stood at our table. And there came the arrogant, cocky, smooth-talking person again. I left the table to go to the loo thinking we were ok, came back to the table, and it was as if I were at a business meeting.

Jesse was very friendly with the waitress, I mean like dead obvious, the one that provokes your red mist to descend. As I sat there, Jesse asked for her mobile number... The flipping cheek. It's so degrading to have someone treat you like that and lay it on so thick to make you flabbergasted, shocked or plain left feeling like a stupid cow. I proceeded to be quiet. I thought it was best whilst my mind was in a flat spin to see if what my eyes had witnessed was real. I went home, Jesse drove with alcohol inside him; I opened the house up and went straight to bed. Still not sure years later, why would I imagine all of that had it not happened as it did? My body was riddled with pain, wearing me down day by day.

I've come back to this place because I did something today to trigger this memory off. In a restaurant, Jesse always found something to moan about. At first, I thought it was because he wanted everything to be perfect for him and me. Silly person that I was, it's something that presented itself in family courts.

Jesse had a flashy lifestyle, and I just simply went along with it. However, Jesse would book extravagant restaurants. It didn't matter where I wanted to go; it was all about him. Sometimes £150 for the two of us was nothing in Jesse's eyes; it was something he could boast and brag about. It started to creep in that, at some point, Jesse would put on his posh voice and ask to see the manager. The very slightest thing would be highlighted and outlined excessively. The manager would offer a free replacement meal and drinks, and Jesse would accept. But it wasn't this at all; what it was is the complaining got him a further income for fancy restaurants for him to laud it up. It's been estimated he made a good £2,000 per year from free meals, drinks and refunds. You may laugh, but he was boasting. You cannot view it another way; this was his plan to deceive. But rest assured, it was a con that worked, and I witnessed him rolling it out time and time again. I got to the point I hated going out with him and apologised where I could.

Jesse would never finish with people unless he had finished playing with them. Toying with their lives in his hands all revealed itself over a period. He would only stop destroying them when he got the ultimate revenge on them. The looks, the stares, the hand gestures; I became fully knowledgeable of what each and all meant. The fear installed into me was spoon-fed to me within a daily routine. Obliviously I became blind to this; piece by piece, the walls were being built around me. Isolating me from my friends and installing into them that I was mentally unwell. He was even taking time to call people to let me know that my brain was sick.

Jesse worked for a very well-known company. He came home one night and, out of the blue, announced he had to go to an awards dinner and escort a colleague. I could not, for love nor money, get it out of him if it were female or male.

In the morning, he received a call. It was a female's voice, so immediately, I thought it was weird, suspicious. Imagine my surprise when I overheard that she had rung him to ensure he'd got everything… Strange! I did not dare open my mouth, but guess what? He still caused a blazing row. I had issues; I was unstable, I was ill… Jesse then stormed off. It's as if he had set the scene for me to react how I did, somehow for him to be less guilty - free to do what he wanted. It all seemed staged, and I had not been very bright. All along, I fell right into what felt like a trap. Every time I would stumble, to be honest, it was a trap; I hadn't imagined it.

That night I didn't expect to hear from him, but he called. The conversation was strained, but I thought it was nice he'd called. Jesse specifically asked me to call him later when he would be in his hotel room. So, when I was asked to call, I called. I'd stayed up late to call him, and the downside was it was midnight when I rang. Silly me, I thought I had got the wrong room, so I made a lame excuse and hung up. I rang the front desk and asked kindly to be put through to his room because I explained I thought I had called someone else's by mistake.

The same voice answered, but this time I asked for Jesse, and she replied, "He's in the shower…"

So, hang on a minute, a female in his room at gone midnight… Nope - I hadn't imagined it. Such red mist time… I asked who she was, and she hung up…

Jesse rang back and was absolutely raging; I mean, off the scale.

"How dare you accuse me? How dare you call? Bitch, you're sick."

Again, I went to bed imaging all sorts… did I really get it so wrong? A little voice inside me said, no, it was what it was. It's only now that it's my belief he had deliberately set me up for me to fall into his traps, and then he was a free person.

Incredibly early in the morning, I was awoken to huge bangs on the front door; the door was bowing with force when I opened it; it was him. Red steam coming out of his ears. His eyes were black, and he looked so angry every line on his face was clearly marked out. Jesse was banging his stuff around. I now realise it is because I had caught him out, but at the time, I didn't want the voice within me to say that out aloud. What was he going to do to me…? My daughters were asleep upstairs, so I did what I could to calm him down. Not the easiest of tasks. I can't imagine what the girls saw, heard or what impact this was having on them. I think the girls and I were in survival mode. I protected them as much as possible, but I doubt it was ever enough now, looking back on reflection.

When someone comes into your life and changes it, I guess it's doubly challenging to walk away from it. When you've never had anyone spoil you, I think deep down you don't want to let go of it. This sounds kind of sick, but hopefully, you might be able to relate to it. I was starting to see friends come and go; I had some great friendships; Karen, Graham, her boys, Lesley, etc., all didn't like Jesse. They tried to tell me, but I guess I wasn't listening. I don't remember being brave. I just remember thinking that everyone should be given a chance to correct their behaviours, or you need to see through your own eyes.

Lesley, a friend of mine for over 21 years, constantly stated what a twat he was. She passed some comments that, when he was friendly, he was a nice bloke, but she always said it's a case of which character turns up.

Chapter Six

Lesley took her own life on 28th December 2018 and left notes for everyone. Including my message that stated to 'Tell the B@@@@@@, I'm dead.' Still, in the lockdown of the pandemic, I haven't fathomed out what she meant. Lesley said what she wanted when she wanted; she didn't give a hoot.

I met her at a Cambridgeshire military base in 2000 when she walked down an aisle with her Welsh voice. You could hear her before you saw her, as a PA to the station commander, bold as brass. Elegantly dressed, Lesley was handing out sweets to the RAF staff as it was her birthday.

I guess they were cheeky as all you could hear was her in that broad Welsh accent, saying, "Go away, you cheeky lot. You won't get a sweet if you carry on!"

She walked straight up to me and stated, "You must be the new kid on the block. Stay away from that lot. Vultures, that lot. Vultures, I tell you."

I knew, from that moment onwards, I had a friend. I knew I could never be the elegant lady she had become, nor could I keep up with her intelligence. But, apart from the other person in my life, we would form a bond. I had an awesome best friend for over two decades; boy, I was a fortunate girl. She's not here, but some days when I look up to the skies, I am sure I see her star shining brightly.

Her last Christmas present to me was a bloody awful cushion. It said on the label, "Something for you to hug." I kept the tag still to this day, and I placed it on our tiny Christmas tree last year.

Karen and Graham worked at the military base, too, with Lesley and me. Wow, what an experience that was. Karen was also Welsh, and she didn't take any prisoners in life; she stood for 0% misbehaviours but was a very clever and funny lady. Her two boys and husband made for a very tight and well-oiled machine that was a fantastic unit. Something I don't think I had witnessed before.

Time goes by so quickly when you think about things; where does a day start and end when it is so blurred and lost? My life with this person takes lots of twists and turns. So, fast-forward from 2001 to 2003, and I was on holiday down in Cornwall for the umptieth time.

The cottages were the family's two two-bedroomed cottages down in a village near Cornwall. It was always a place that was his and mine to escape to. It was a tranquil location with a view that one day would be shared between the four of us, Maud (Jesse's sister), Toby (Jesse's brother-in-law), Jesse and myself. I was expected to clean, cook, and repair these properties and treat them as my own, which is precisely what I did.

The locals all knew Jesse and me because Jesse would be shouting and boasting, and I would apologise for his destructive behaviours. Funny how it all worked out - he would go out, I would walk back alone, down the dirt tracks back to the cottages, go to bed on my own again. I'd been going there for years because I was constantly told they would be ours one day and it would be part of my pension if I played my cards right. If I toed the line of keeping quiet, I would end up with them.

For years, I have cleaned, repaired, painted, took bookings and telecom calls, and spent weeks doing the gardening because my mother-in-law said I would always be part of this family. I assumed all the encouragement to be truthful. I spent years working like a Trojan.

At first, I did it because I was always asked by Jesse. After all, he said we would inherit them. "They are ours in the future."

I also want to say very clearly that I love a tidy house and have been brought up to clean up after myself and leave a place how I found it. I was constantly cleaning and ensuring it was suitable for all the paying customers. Just as if it were my own home, but I want to park these comments now, and I'll come back to it.

On one visit to Cornwall, I was pregnant with Jesse's baby, and we went with Nicola and Jason, Jesse's friends. They had known him for years, especially Jason. He knew Jesse inside out and basically didn't put up with his verbal rubbish.

Jesse wanted me to eliminate the "problem." He wasn't ready on several levels; I'd tricked him, etc. He even threw money to get rid of the issue; I can't remember him once referring to it as his baby – it was always my baby. However, he did state he would support me and help me deal with it. Looking back, I distinctly remember feeling lower than low.

I gave in to all the hassle, screaming, and got rid of the baby. Jesse took me and brought me back.

He or she would have been 17/18 now, and I often wonder what they would have been like. So many people out there can't have children. I was getting rid of one, and I didn't want to dispose of this little baby. It felt like taking a picture off the wall and throwing it in the bin in Jesse's eyes; no connection to emotion. In mine, it was devastating, very distressing and shameful. I was so alone only four people knew I was pregnant.

When the baby was terminated, I was supposed to tell people that I had lost it or had to get rid of it because Jesse didn't want a child. I remember my mind wandering on what could have been, but I quickly knew to keep the peace to shove it all back in a box and sit on the lid. I always remember the guilt I felt that my mind would feel, yet my heart told me something else. They didn't speak the same language; why didn't they?

Even to this day, it's detached as I struggle to get back on track. My current excellent counsellor says that it isn't abnormal when you're in this situation. So, don't punch yourself; it's normal to become detached, don't think about self-harming yourself; it's good that you know that.

When something like this happened, I used to butcher my toes, I mean slay them. Savagely rip my toenails out, make them bleed, get infections of all sorts. This is possibly the first time I've ever let anyone in on this; it's something I kept very secret. But there are no more secrets now. There were days I couldn't walk, shoes wouldn't fit, but I hid it well for an exceptionally long time. It sounds sick now, but I wouldn't have stopped for anyone or anything unless I saw blood and felt great pain.

Thank goodness in 2019, I stopped and recognised why I was doing it… I was self-harming to escape and distract myself from what was really going on around me and my girlies. I can honestly say I do it considerably less than I used to and go long periods of not doing it at all. I view this as a massive positive, and I am proud that I got the issue out when I was ready to come clean about how bad I felt regarding certain things.

I awoke one morning, and my left arm was numb. At first, I thought I had slept on it funny. Let's be honest; we have all done it.

I had to go to the doctor's a day or so later as the pain was horrendous. They gave me painkillers and sent me on my way; three weeks later, the pain still rising, I went back. I was given more pain killers, the size of horse pills; however, my arm had become very cold and purple. I couldn't sleep, and it was awful.

I returned to the doctor's two weeks later and said I couldn't cope with the pain anymore. I was referred to see one specialist after another with no explanation of what was wrong with my arm.

In the end, Jesse paid for me to go privately; I now remember thinking about all the trouble my arm was causing our relationship. I was a burden, psychosomatic; the name-calling was an onslaught. I knew something serious was wrong, and it was best I said nothing. It was causing endless rows over how much pain I was in; it was me stopping him from going out. It was me who was a bore; it was me that had an ugly arm that he was looking at. I am convinced he would strike that arm for the slightest thing I did to ensure I was in maximum pain. He would always state he had forgotten it was my bad arm.

I ended up having four (in total) surgeries to save my left arm. These included having the shoulder bone shaved and cleaned up first, then the ligaments stitched back together, then back in again to repair more inside stuff. These ops were to no avail, so they went back in and removed my first rib. They found out that I had a rare illness called Thoracic Outlet Syndrome (TOS). It wasn't all in my head, and more importantly, I had a full diagnosis to prove that I hadn't imagined any of this. I am just grateful that my arm returned to function after 11 months of not working.

I had obviously buried this issue, yet I did something today, and it all came to the surface again. It linked to the name-calling about my freaky arm to anyone who would listen to Jesse. Why say something nice when you can easily say something horrid without thinking it through? I would never raise this with him; otherwise, that would have been another prod or poke on my very sore arm. I used to sweat. I was in that much pain, lengthy rehab sessions, but I got my left arm working again. TOS is a condition that traps the workings of the arm and, in some cases, eventually causes things to snap.

I returned to work with some adaptions, and since then, fingers crossed, I haven't endured any severe issues with my left arm.

Chapter Seven

So, in 2005, when I was caught being pregnant again, there was no way I would dispose of another beautiful baby. I was 11 weeks gone before I noticed, mainly because I never had periods, got sick and before I knew it, I've tested positive. I didn't once think that I would be blessed with another opportunity of a lifetime. This baby was not going anywhere.

By the time I told Jesse, I was 12 weeks pregnant.

His face initially dropped, but as time went on, he kept saying things like, "Who's the daddy? I'm the daddy!"

Jesse went to Asda's and did some food shopping and came back with a T-shirt for me. My bump would have been around 15 weeks by this time. Within a week or so, we would be attending the maternity clinic to see if everything was ok. I was focused on the baby, but Jesse was more focused on me wearing that T-shirt whenever there was going to be an audience.

When Jesse and I attended the maternity clinic, we got to see our beautiful baby with its long legs and long body. The nurse let us know there was a baby there and said everything looked ok. Jesse's face crashed from what looked like a half-hearted smile became a total gutted reaction; the baby was real. Jesse walked out of the room, and I was close behind him; however, he drove off and left me at the hospital. I called him repeatedly and eventually got him to come back and pick us up. I didn't know whether to flip out or just reassure him.

I kept a baby diary, and I hope Lexie will read it when she's older and decide for herself what the truth is through her eyes. I don't think

I can even begin to describe his fear or reactions to the news that he would become a father.

My father-in-law Charles loved the news, his face looking excited at another grandchild. However, the dreadful Smother had a look like she'd eaten a bag of sour lemons. Maybe the attention wouldn't have been on her. Was she jealous? Was she hacked off because, for the following months, it would not have been all about her?

Then bang - there you go, the bag of lemon's face spoke out… "It will have to be a boy as my Jesse Poo's wouldn't be having a girl. His sperm is potent for boys."

What's that got to do with the price of fish? OMG, what a comment. Why say something nice when you can say something horrid? A horrible, disgusting woman - she might have married into money, but she still talks like she's from the council estate she grew up in. Bitter and twisted, what made her like this?

My mind's exhausted, thinking about why the prospective grandma wouldn't be happy. The same Smother that once smacked one of my daughters on holiday (her step-granddaughter).

Jealousy is weird to understand, but with Grandma being in her 70's, "Where was the threat?" I mean, seriously. There is no threat; she's a princess from a council house, the big I am with the big I am nothing.

I went to my first maternity appointment at the local hospital. I was super excited; I had great boobs, a little bump, and today, I saw the baby on the screen. Jesse was nowhere as enthusiastic as me; he constantly looked like a rabbit caught in headlights.

Jesse's face dropped; he told the nurse he was convinced he would always have a boy! "I can't believe I'm going to have a girl". Jesse looked and acted totally gutted she was a girl.

He further cemented my concerns by storming off the maternity wing and drove off and left me there.

This wasn't the first time he stormed off and left me stranded, but I honestly thought he would have mellowed to the concept because I was pregnant with his baby. After sex without contraception, undoubtedly, who knows what might happen next? Clearly not singing from the same hymn sheet, were we?

I think I bought shame to the father's family by having a girl; they didn't seem happy. Well, hang on, hang on; *one* family member didn't seem satisfied. The Smother just wouldn't accept that her future grandchild was going to be a girl. I said I would have a DNA test if she felt like that. At the time, the Jeremy Kyle TV show was offering people these tests to shut them up. Fourteen years later, OMG, you can tell she has their genes.

The strange shape of the big toe is the thing that connects Charles, Maud, Jesse, and Lexie together. She has amazing red hair that shines beautiful colours, but she had no hair at all to start with. It seemed she would never have any at one point, but the red hair is like the Smother-in-Law's.

I went to work and decided to tell some people our news. Many of my colleagues were all jumping for joy, hugs, and tears of sheer enjoyment. However, my close friend Karen also broke her news. It turns out we were about a month apart with our delivery dates. My eldest daughters were so pleased and rubbed my bump a lot. Their faces lit up like a thousand lights at Blackpool. It was great to share my happiness with friends at work, but a shame that it was one of the only places I distinctly remember chatting about it all. Other than with my parents, it was a rare opportunity to let rip and be freely happy.

I remember being at work, and my bump was so big that I was standing so far away to press the buttons on the photocopier - I should have used a stick. But when I looked right, Karen stood in another row of desks to send a facsimile... in the same situation. It was so funny we both giggled so much we became best friends. Karen and I spent our time at work sharing updates, leaky boobs and needing the loo as everyday conversations.

I don't know why, but I have to come back to this bit because I need to mention the torment of name-calling regarding the development of the baby girl inside me. As you know, your body shape changes to adapt to this amazing experience. Yet the dad constantly pulls you down, whether in front of people or behind closed doors. Normally all the secrets of your private life are all behind closed doors. You're too ashamed to say what's really happening for fear of not being believed, or you fear worse will happen to you from speaking out.

Jesse took me to Cornwall at the end of July 2005 as he said it would possibly be our last holiday without a baby. I didn't have much energy for anything, nothing fitted, and I was the size of a whale taken from Sea World in Florida. From the time I got up every morning, I waited on hand and foot on the expectant father all day, so I was tired. I cleaned the cottage down as if we hadn't been there, but to be honest, I think it had something to do with the famous dressing gown issues. I had gradually noticed the dressing gown issues creeping into my life more and more.

Jesse would get up naked, always put on a dressing gown and not sit very covered up. Let's be open; downstairs on a man or woman isn't the prettiest of things to look at, so imagine first thing in the morning, legs sort of crossed to flash their bits at you. Not a pretty sight, but the dressing gown issue became a concern further into my life to the point it destroyed everything.

So, you're on holiday, supposedly having relaxation time between you and your baby's father, yet you are working hard and long hours. The cottage was clean, and guess who was still in the dressing gown at 12:05 pm? Yes, you've got it, despite my best efforts to actively encourage him that we should go out for a nice walk. He had to have a shower and get ready, which for a bald person took hours. He often used to wash downstairs with a back to front action and turned himself on. Then we would have to wait for him to towel dry himself, and being honest with me, I had felt that we were losing valuable time to enjoy Cornwall.

This day it was 2.03 pm before we had even left the cottage, so I was frustrated, and it must have shown.

But this person had started to show me that I wasn't essential or heard with my "Come on love, let us go and do something" request.

I was literally walking up and down the dales - in Cornwall, there are a few steep declines and inclines when you walk across the fields. By the time we arrived in the town centre, I was cream crackered and tired, with fat ankles, and I needed a wee, etc. He played up the whole time, wanting to go in every shop - not to spend, but just to browse. Maybe this is a time to clarify Jesse demanded to go into every shop. Even though I wanted to go to Boots to get something for my swollen feet to cool them down, well, he kicked off. I left Boots in total embarrassment and ran to the exit. I asked to go back to the cottage, which resulted in another argument in the street.

Eventually, we went to the taxi rank near the cinema and went back. Silence and huff and puffing in the taxi made it difficult; I didn't answer back too much because I was trapped in a cab and in fear of his anger.

When we got to the cottage, I went into the bedroom. I wept, partly in disbelief, but I was also gutted. I remember thinking, "What have I done, getting pregnant with this person?" We didn't speak for the rest of the night; he drank and drank, and I stayed in the bedroom.

When I awoke, the mess in the kitchen was terrible; he'd made himself a midnight snack, left everything everywhere. I started to tidy it up, but obviously, he continued to scream at me because, lo and behold, he had a bad hangover. I placed 11 bottles of beer in the bins and made too much noise. Part of me just wanted to escape, and part of me wanted to scream back at him. It seems I did both on reflection; I packed my suitcase and left after saying what I needed to say. He was in his dressing-gown, making out it was all my fault and that I had caused all of it. Maybe I had; I was pregnant and just tagging along to provide for Jesse. When all along, I thought it was for me to put my feet up and be spoilt like I had been told.

I dragged that suitcase, which was awkward, to say the least, but I headed for the train station in Hayle, which I believed to have been about 5 miles away. He eventually came to find me and the bump, but I didn't want to know; I just wanted to go home. For me, it had been a total waste of my time when I only asked for a compromise in some areas. I was sold on the idea that the holiday was for me to relax and be spoilt. Not for a minute did I think it was for the other way round. Yet little did I know I would be frogmarched across the hills in Cornwall and expected to stand there whilst he bought what he wanted.

When I would rest, Jesse would say nasty words for me to get up. Jesse would be singing the song from B52's; the line in the song is "It's as big as a whale, and it's about to set sail." Referencing my size, I wasn't that big at this stage of the pregnancy, but I did feel larger than I looked.

He drove his car very erratically but demanded I get in the car. Being pressured to stop embarrassing myself, he promised to take me home that day. He returned to the cottage and said I was ridiculous and making a spectacle of myself, and it wasn't good for the baby. I backed down after he went on and on about my behaviour and its effect on her.

The following morning, we returned to the West Midlands rather silently, but I preferred it, if I am honest.

Chapter Eight

I worked right up until the baby was born - almost quite literally. Karen was overdue to give birth by two weeks. I was four weeks behind her; however, Karen delivered a beautiful baby on Monday 29th August 2005, a girl she called Ella.

On that Wednesday, 31st August, I finished work, with a big send-off of gifts to go with my waddling. God, I felt huge but in love with my baby girl all at the same time. I collected a brand-new car and purchased a new mobile phone on Thursday, so I had a new car to put our beautiful baby girl into and my new mobile to take beautiful pictures of her. I had plenty of time to set everything up now I was on maternity leave.

So, what do you think went wrong? Yes, you've guessed right - my waters broke at 05:00 am. She's early, OMG! What am I going to do? I asked Jesse to get up and get ready to take us to the hospital. Jesse took the mickey out of my waters leaking; he screeched on two wheels all the way to the hospital. It was a terrifying journey; I didn't even know if I would make it there alive! He was furious - as if I could stop our baby from coming; she was coming, and that's it. Why doesn't he just find the courage and get on with the situation? He's going to become a dad. Why wasn't he excited? The rabbit's head in headlights was back, a grown person yet an absolute baby.

His toddler behaviour drove me up the wall and the nurses who were around me too. Instead of him being concerned about our baby, he was acting the goat. He was told to get changed into some blues ready for theatre because I had to have an emergency Caesarean to get her out.

So, there I am, being drugged and prepped for theatre. There he is with no underwear on and these thin blue surgeon clothes, prancing around with a stethoscope, acting as if he is the surgeon.

He was shouting down the corridor to another expectant mother; he informed her that I was a pain and would get to her as quick as he could! This pregnant mother was waiting to be seen. What should have been a happy time was diminished as Jesse behaved like a demanding brat again! Yelling down the corridor as if he was a proper doctor and was telling the truth. I can see precisely how errors happen in the hospital; I had asked him to stop clowning around all to no avail. Not even on the day his daughter was due could Jesse step up to the plate.

Our baby girl was born beautifully safe and sound; however, I became gravely ill for a short while but soon recovered when the doctors got me back. I had many internal and external stitches. My mum came to the hospital and was so pleased; however, the nightmare demanded to see her grandchild too, and my mum kindly disappeared.

So, hang on a minute; my mum drove 140 miles to come and know that we are both ok, and the Smother-in-Law lives 10 mins away, but it's my mother that was forced to leave. The Smother-in-Law took one look at her biological grandchild and stated that Wendy would have made an excellent mum. All whilst I was in the hospital in pain.

God, looking back, I was in so much pain and disappointed, angry all at the same time. Jesse went and wet the baby's head tradition, and I stayed with our new baby girl in hospital. She was beautiful, just like my other two daughters, who now had a little sister to spoil.

Jesse had been living with one foot in and one foot out, in the sense of non-committal. Jesse only lived with my girls and me when he felt like it. What I mean is, it's as if Jesse manufactured an argument to give him the freedom to go home and do what he wanted when he wanted. I fell into this trap on many occasions. I guess the truth is that I didn't see it at the time, but I do now. I have learnt all the holes and bumps I have hit very clearly now.

When I was still in the maternity wing with our daughter, Jesse moved himself in on the day I was coming home. It's as if I had something more than him in a physical sense, and Jesse wasn't going to let me hold any of the cards. I hope this makes sense. As I read it several times, I know what I mean to say. As I am emptying my brain of the events I am trying to recall, they are just stumbling out. I remember each flashback or a trigger, but I can't always work out what they all mean.

Still, to this day, since May 2001, I believe I have been struggling with flashbacks and triggers.

It was supposed to be about my three daughters. The baby, as she was known for a couple of days, gave her big sisters, Alexa and Lucille, presents as they cuddled and smiled at her. They were both accommodating with everything from day one.

So, with the baby born, guess who decided to take the plunge and move in the day I came out of the hospital? Everything was a little upside down because of a newborn, yet on top of that, there was his crap all over the place. He had decided, seeing as we had a child together, he'd better move in.

I had always stated that Jesse had one foot in the relationship and one foot playing it safe. I personally believe Jesse had a plan. Was I in it, and nothing was going to stop him? Was Jesse keeping his options open?

The downside is that it has taken me nearly 20 years to escape the mindset I developed; brainwashing is the better-known wording. I have learnt to mirror his behaviours; I've learnt to hide, transfer a question into a dismissive, vague answer. I would watch television for company and distractions. I've become a circus act at being able to walk on eggshells, avoiding his temper, his demands, yet I survived nothing in some ways. A life of friendships disappeared one by one, a dash of not being seen in public. I became the expert in avoiding everything to ensure life would be smoother; then, I became the one to portray the same thing for protecting my babies.

Both Alexa and Lucille were awesome babies, and they are amazing women now. All grown up and have children of their own.

When the baby came home, who was a quiet one 95% of the time, someone behaved like a fish out of the water, flapping about everywhere. Jesse was only ever with her when someone was nearby, and the first time she would cry, Jesse would kick off. She was only picked up by her father when someone came to see her - a shame, but unfortunately true. I never knew who to try and keep quiet, the adult or the baby.

One day, God knows what had kicked off, but Jesse screamed at the top of the stairs; I was a slut! It came from nowhere, but Alexa heard everything. Still, to this day, I have no idea what I had done wrong - if anything at all. I wrote a diary on my pregnancy just to support myself where I could.

So, the baby's name was decided by all of us, Alexa, Lucille, Jesse and me, by putting names in Jesse's hat, and the first name we pulled out would be her name. The hat was an Australian one, big and bold, just like someone's ego. Alexa chose Mollie, Lucille chose Millie, Jesse chose Tabatha, and I chose Lexie. This is how Lexie's first name was decided. There wasn't any discussion on her middle name (Ursula) because it was selected months before after attending a marriage ceremony in Germany with Andy and Ursula. It's fair to say that Lexie detests it.

One night I asked Jesse to bathe her, the one night which has scarred her for life. Lexie moved around in the bath and somehow bashed her eyebrow on the tap edge. I then heard this almighty scream, a harrowing one. Jesse didn't know what to do, so I placed her up wrapped her in a large towel. I grabbed a nappy and took a short trip to the hospital A & E. Jesse obviously wasn't watching her properly, seeing as he was on the telephone to his mate… grrr.

They glued her eye and said they wouldn't refer this to the Social Services as clearly it was an accident. Lexie has a permanent scar on her eyebrow, but being a girl means she can disguise it. Not the answer, but hey, there's always some positive from a negative.

I was at work one day, and I usually did everything for everyone, every morning, every day. There was one day that Jesse argued with me, but I don't know why. I just got the heck out of there, scooping all the girls up too. I dropped Lucille off at school, Alexa walked to school, and Lexie had to go to nursery. I had the silent treatment all day as Jesse refused to answer his phone. I apologised to smooth things over for whatever I had done, but being honest, I had no recollection of what it was.

I finished work and went to the nursery, but Lexie had been taken from there earlier. They explained that Jesse had taken her, but the panic set in, that sick, heavy feeling that doesn't ever leave you. I tried desperately to contact him, wanting to know why Jesse had done this. Don't worry; I quickly realised this was to punish and torture me. The thought of ringing the police did come to my mind, but I know they wouldn't have done anything as we lived as man and wife. Jesse was such a liar that he was believable. I know Jesse would have said anything plausible to release himself from suspicion.

Jesse would have said I was a nutter, deranged and suffering from some sick illness. "Once again, she didn't listen to what I said when I left for work."

It was always my fault; maybe I was strong enough to shoulder the blame and take responsibility for all the bad behaviour. One thing's for sure, at the start of it, I was mentally stronger. That's not the case now; I'm a bedraggled wreck. I'm like a pencil with no lead in it, empty. I just exist in a life I can't escape from. Even years later, it is still the case.

I think Jesse thought Lexie was a pawn he could use to get at me. I don't believe that anymore. I know she is a pawn to him. Jesse has no feelings, emotions or recollection of situations. Jesse has forgotten his Smother, who is, in my eyes, a "Bad bitch breeds bad pups" - the total centre of all of this. I did some research this year, and how true is that? It comes from the mother, and it's passed down to the next generation. Spooky but allegedly true.

I always wondered why I was his target practice; I asked why I was left with the baby, and his life never altered once. It took him ages to sell the two-seater Audi. I didn't ever allow Lexie to go into his car because Jesse drove like a maniac. As an adult, I loved fast driving, but Jesse even scared me most times. Looking back, I can't remember him taking her for a walk in the pram. I have no memories that Jesse gave up attending a pub quiz for her. Strange but true.

43

Wow, all the memories of sadness, hurt, anger, doubt, a sequence of events had even happened – do my memories twist the truth? What were the facts? Well, I don't know anything anymore. I'm just the dumb person trying to make sense, not only of my life but the girls' lives too.

My two older daughters have not had life easy; firstly, their father and I split up. Phil was a kind person and my best mate too; we married so young, and it's a travesty it didn't work out. None of this was their fault; in fact, they were victims too in this holocaust.

My eldest daughter grew up with Jesse relentlessly taking the mick out of her teeth, name-calling, and anything else to reduce her to tears. They did get on some of the time; Alexa was an amazing daughter who never caused her biological father or me any issues. However, her step-father thought his banter was character-building for her. I didn't see it that way because the strength of his banter was as forceful as a tsunami. The storm pulls you back and then ramps up, to then hit you with a massive effect. Knocking you over, drowning you, suffocating every breath and gulp of air you take. There's a song that comes to mind, "I get knocked down, but I get up again; you're never going to keep me down." I doubt that. One day I won't get up; my energy for life keeps disappearing. It worries me that I would leave this world not knowing how life would eventually turn out. But why live for something that you hate so much, with blame, regret etc., etc.?

Lucille, the middle daughter, is beautiful inside and out, talented, clever, and has an endless sense of humour. On many occasions, I have looked over my shoulder. I can see she suffered from his rubbish too. Maybe I wasn't there to protect her to the best of my ability, either. Is this why I feel like the worst mother in the world?

I had three quite different children and a blooming mess of an adult who was more childish than the kids. I say this, feeling incredibly stressed and with tears in my eyes: Alexa, Lucille, Lexie and Him. Yes, I include him because, most of the time, I was pandering to his needs above and beyond when all I should have been focusing on was the girlies, first and foremost. Despite having a toddler and two teenagers, a full-time job with the Ministry of Defence and a house to maintain, he took all my time. I never felt relaxed, and I always lived on my nerves, but I thought it was because I just couldn't manage my time or something. Again, I would look in a mirror and think it's all my fault, and I'll address it later. The trouble is that the later stage has never happened yet.

Chapter Nine

In 2006, I approached a solicitor for legal advice on removing Jesse from my house. I couldn't cope: I feared for things around me, and the threats of Lexie being removed drove me insane with panic. I couldn't live like this anymore; I needed someone else to see this through their eyes to judge what was going on. As I call it, the fog or haze was me knowing something was wrong but not having the strength to identify the path to escape. The letter issued to Jesse was a shot across the bow, but not for long; he soon came into line and back into our lives.

Those sad puppy eyes, "I was only joking, Hun, you take life far too seriously…"

This letter to this day is still circulating. Don't worry about another. I will come back to it.

Jesse and I got married in Barbados in August 2007; it was a beautiful occasion, I mean stunning. There was a Category 4 hurricane the night before the ceremony. I had a wet wedding dress floating in a box across the room when I woke up. Gutted and panic-stricken, I found someone to dry it out; three hairdryers later, it was brought back dry. Phew, I was so relieved.

I surprised the hell out of everyone on the day because, for at least seven days before the wedding, no one saw me dressed up or with my hair done. I mean hat, bikini, sunglasses all the time look, in the sea, out the sea. I deliberately dressed myself down for maximum impact on the wedding day.

On the day, the hotel staff were fantastic, got all the chairs and tables out and turned it around. It was a stunning setting, but I guess I look back now and feel that we only got married so he could have rights. Not sure at this stage what it is I am trying to say. I may come back to this if I remember what haze came over me after that day.

We came home from the wedding in Barbados and had another celebration at an 800-year-old castle/hotel in the West Midlands. Again, it was a stunning location; it was also the day of my 40th, so it classed as a double celebration. I had another eventful start to the morning as I had hired a Del Boy lookalike and the yellow van as my wedding car. Del Boy's real name was Maurice, and he rang me in the morning to arrange what time he would be coming. The downside was Jesse answering the phone; this was supposed to be a surprise. So, I made out the horse and cart were ready to take me to the hotel but made out one of the horses was sick. He didn't know it was all about the surprise for him.

I was collected by Maurice, and you couldn't tell the difference from Del Boy - OMG, spitting image! We parked up in a hidden estate near the hotel; the van had a blow-up doll and a cone on top, just like the TV programme. The van owner started it up, and it was backfiring, smoking etc., just like the real thing that we all watched as children.

Then, disaster struck. Someone in the estate called the police… Yeah, they did. So, I am in my wedding dress with Del Boy. Well, the police fell about laughing when they pulled up. Some miserable sod was upset by the van backfiring. The police had photos next to Del Boy and the van. I bet the station loved the story. I was told that the police were in trouble for being late back, but I promised them copies of the pictures.

So, I got in the van, the police drove off, and we headed for the 900m castle driveway. At the bottom were selected guests laughing their socks off at the van coming down the hill. Little did they know I was in it; everyone was waiting for the horse and cart! Del Boy is Jesse's favourite. Maurice stepped out shouting, "I've got my Raquel in the car!"

A hilarious day went beautifully, but it should have done. Jesse and I spent over £30k on it. Jesse mainly paid for it, but I paid where I could. We had horse racing games on a screen and prizes; however, some people got highly competitive, and we had to make horses fall as a result, lol. The England final was on, of course; we had an artist that drew characters badly on purpose, bouncy castles etc. - just lots of fun.

As time has gone by, I can't remember any happier memories than this day. Karen and Graham left incredibly early; let's be honest, it was because of me and the girls they were there. Alexa and Lucille were stunning on the run-up to the wedding and afterwards. I do distinctively remember beautiful memories of getting the girls' dresses with them. Seeing them all dressed up and with their hair done was beautiful. I will not forget those smiles and images until the day I pass over.

Married life wasn't all it was cracked up to be, for the second time for me. Jesse would state he needed to work hard to recover the wedding cost, which I remember was a clear way to disguise his comings and goings. I never knew where I was with him. So, part of me would become frustrated at being dumped on, and part of me needed him to help me out. I felt abandoned yet needy. Does that make sense? I cannot explain myself very well because I didn't like him, yet I guess there was love at some point. I think he loved himself, hidden and deceitful to the maximum.

I had a fantastic career in the MOD, seeing as I had "come from nothing," according to the Smother-in-Law. I left school wanting to become England's best gymnast and didn't focus on my education, which would have got me there. I spent years perfecting my craft in ten years of ballet and ten years of gymnastics; Loughborough University formed my training and coaching.

Yet in the Brown's household, through my awful Smother-in-law's eyes, I was constantly reminded how it was nice "her son had rescued me from the gutter." It's not funny how some disgusting comments play on a loop in your brain to the point you never forget the wording. How could I forget when it was told to me on most weeks and days? How could I be me?

I had been told that I had come from a Gypsy family background, so let me explain. My nanna was well to do in the Army, but the Smother-in-Law had significantly better stories; her uncle was this and that. It shouldn't have been a competition, oh, but it was with her! What she doesn't seem to remember is that she came from a council house environment and married into a significant amount of money. No wonder Charles was browbeaten; you never once heard him brag, boast or be disrespectful. I believe that people who are born with money, you would never know, but people who acquire it become sick and greedy. I bet as you read this, you can relate to it.

My mum and dad did ok in life; Dad had a very well-known garage. He was a stock car driver and in a band in the '70s; he was exceptionally good at it and well known. Mum was excellent at tennis, hockey, baking and horses, so where had I come from a Gypsy background? But don't worry, this comes up repeatedly in my later life.

I understood how sick the relationships were around me at this point but still thought it wouldn't happen to me. I remember how she brought out the worst in me at times as I wanted to defend myself and be heard, but it would have had repercussions. Keep your gob shut. Elizabeth never seemed to work, yet slowly but surely, I was hating going to the Smother-in-Law's house. I couldn't compete with her; I didn't want to.

I also go to the point of thinking, with evidence in front of me, that Lexie wasn't mentally safe there either. I guess what I am trying to say is that Lexie was being picked on and ridiculed. Let me explain further. Lexie was born with no hair; she also had a lot of what could be perceived to be red in her skin. There were a lot of discussions that Lexie wasn't Jesse's. I so dearly wanted Lexie's dad to defend not only me but his daughter. I can't say Lexie is his only child because I have suspicions there is another secret child, but I could be wrong. As Lexie was growing up, the Smother-in-Law seemed to be fighting for attention.

At Christmas parties, people would make a fuss of Lexie, and I guess the Smother felt excluded. But gradually, I noticed that each time Lexie was near her, there were secret comments and telephone conversations. As Lexie was growing up, her hair began to grow, and at the time, it was a gorgeous colour, red. Fine, spikey hair to start with that shone in so many different reds and dark blondes. She was a showstopper; she had wide blue eyes, red hair and fantastic skin. She was always smiling and a happy baby, but I noticed she wouldn't go to her grandma over time. Alexa and Lucille were also becoming aware of her not wanting to go to the Smother-in-Law's house either.

Why would a toddler protest at seeing her grandma? Papa was awesome with Lexie; he played the piano, and she always went to him. Their relationship was such that Papa and Lexie were in awe of each other. If Lexie wanted a drink at the Smother-in-Law's, she had to say, "Nana, darling, please can I have a drink?" before she would get one.

Bear in mind, whenever she went shopping or out of the house, upon her return, she would bellow, "Papa doodles, Mummy's home…" He was in his 70's, for goodness' sake. His other name was "Colly Wolly." Yes, you're right; it's pathetic and a little bit sick. What's wrong with just saying a simple "I am home?"

All the nicknames were, in my opinion, a form of childish chitchat. Calling their son "Jesse Poo's" at 37 years old seemed very odd, never mind the other names being bandied around. It was funny how Maud, Jesse's sister, didn't have a name other than Maud. She was nice to start with and seemed to argue a lot with her mother. Sulks and tantrums came into the beam of lights when Maud and her mother were in the room.

One day at a barbecue at Maud's old house, the mother stormed off - so infantile. I know that Maud got the silent treatment for a couple of weeks, but now Maud is becoming her mother's double. Jacob Harold, Maud's only child, was a lovely boy, ginger-haired and subjected to awful incidents by the mother-in-law and Jesse. Name-calling, "Gay. Get your teeth fixed. Get your hair cut, you yeti." It continued relentlessly and, at times, was even worse.

He was only allowed to have full-fat milk and was treated like a toddler despite being a young person. He didn't have many choices to study at his pace; he was pushed and pushed to be better. In addition to that, he constantly had to do test papers, wasn't allowed an opinion, a break, or any voice that I had witnessed. I didn't like that he was pressured so much; I also thought that Jacob Harold needed to find his own path, not what someone else wanted for him. At every opportunity, he was packed off to boarding schools during the holidays at his grandparents.

I felt for him. I thought I had seen these behaviours all before. I also saw a clear picture of things around me yet felt I had lead weights on my feet to leg it. I also started to withdraw; sometimes, you couldn't get a word out of me and other times, you couldn't shut me up. It would spill out and take me back to the episodes where my emotions felt like Victoria Falls. My current counsellor lets me cascade and spill out; I'm yet to stop. I am more nervous because I can't stop. Even if I wanted to pause at the halt sign, I could not seem to find the brakes. I nervously worry that I am boring her, going over old ground; it's clearly all very messed up in my head.

Chapter Ten

In 2008 I applied for a job in Germany in an Army HQ; I spoke with everyone who mattered and went for it. Working in a new country isn't as bad as it seems if you have support. The support I had around me was pointless at the time. I went over for my interviews and returned to the news to find out that I had the job.

Packing up the house with children to move abroad was an exciting venture. A big but in all of this was all the glory coming from Jesse's mouth; it was him that had accomplished this achievement. I quickly became aware that it wasn't about what I could do. It was about making me ensure he was on a pedestal. It was an opportunity for him to become a loud, brash person with no common courtesy that his wife arrived at this fabulous opportunity.

I arrived in December with Lexie, and it was blooming freezing; the winters are awfully long and cold. With the job, I received a house to live in and MOD furniture, incredibly old-fashioned, but great that they did this for us. I kept the house in the West Midlands and ran whilst I did three years with the British Army in Germany. I was a boss of a German person, I had massive responsibilities, and I think I was thriving on it. I took my car over to Germany, but it became a significant concern of mine when Jesse came over to join us. Over the years of being with Jesse, I realised that he would thrash my car to bits when I wasn't in it. He also drove at high speeds, even with the girls and me in it. Over time, I absolutely hated it; it made me see red, yet I struggled to comprehend why it would make me so angry. But

I think it is because I took tremendous pride in my car's appearance; I hoovered and washed it regularly. I drove it carefully because I had my three girls to think about. It wasn't always about my safety; it was about them being in the car too. I was a mother, for God's sake. My car became a concern when Jesse would ever borrow it. He always drove like an idiot. If he wanted to do that in his, fine, but not in someone else's. Where was the respect?

In Germany, one day, I had a senior military guy pull me into his office. It transpired that Jesse had driven my car down the main drag of a military street and clocked over 3,000 euros in speeding fines. This disgraced the military unit within Germany, and it wasn't fair on me: the distrust and the discourteous behaviour. I took the rollicking as best as I could. I was told to bring my husband into line, or I would face punishments too.

So, I paid the fines and went home to tell Jesse the news; he laughed as if he had just got a new trophy. This was a memorable moment because I realised my career was starting to become spoilt.

I had such unique experiences in Germany; I met Gavin and his family, who is still my best mucker to this day. I went to Defence Attachés homes, the Czech Republic, NATO Offices and received awards; oh my goodness, the credits just kept rolling. The summers were so hot and surrounded by your own family (the military families). The winters were -28ºC. Boy, did you need to sleep with your socks on! Digging the snow from the driveways and paths is not something I will miss. It was deep, heavy snow - when it fell, it fell.

Unfortunately, I had to have a minor operation on my right shoulder in November 2009; this was cancelled as I had a nasty cold.

The op was rescheduled for the 19th of January 2010. This is the date when Edward Scissorhands (a military surgeon) cut something inside my shoulder he shouldn't have. I was back on the ward for a couple of days and in a terrible way. Somehow, I had lost the use of my right arm and leg.

I had to go back into theatre twice. I had a severed right lung and a blood clot. When I woke for the third time, there was still no function in my right arm and leg. I found myself becoming scared, but I remember Gavin bringing me Burger King meals and smiles. I lost many muscles and ligaments on the right side, and I had every element of looking like a stroke victim.

Jesse came and brought Lexie to come and see me, but it was loud and disruptive. Jesse wasn't kind and seemed incredibly angry, as if I had caused this myself. I was made to feel I was a burden; I was often called names. Going to the toilet, I was assisted by nurses, then Jesse. It wasn't an easy situation. I remember being pulled about over these years, roughly treated, grabbed, or left to fend for myself. I guess I was scared, worried and learning German very quickly to get a nurse to the bedside. Don't you just love a crash course in German medical speech!

In 2016 I had a remote prognosis that became clear. It was a nasty condition called CRPS Type II (Complex Regional Pain Syndrome) in the damaged right arm. So, when I explain this later, you will relate to this bit. The arm and right hand sweated excessively, and Jesse never wanted to hold my hand. If it sweated, he would take the piss out of me, but despite my patient responses and deep breaths, I still held on to my tongue. In addition to this, when it did sweat, it meant I was in horrific pain. I even asked a surgeon to cut the arm off as I had been driven that far with the pain. Sometimes there was pain coming from my heart, but it was mostly my head and the home life. The more stress I was under, the more my conditions resulted in pain. Whenever my arm was knocked or firmly touched, it hurt like hell for days, weeks, months.

I used to sit still if I possibly could whilst the swelling and heat inside the arm calmed down. I used to be questioned about what I had been doing all day. You can imagine I couldn't do much with a pointless right arm and leg, breathing like a pit bull with a squashed nose. My lung seemed to take forever to repair, and I had plenty of physio to forget which bit hurt the most. I had a tough time recovering from pain and regaining the usage of my limbs and organs. It also influenced the court hearing for clinical negligence. My so-called husband decided to not negotiate fairly with the Army but more took on the war. Sometimes I was forced to take options I didn't want to take. It was easier.

Since my injuries, it has taken me 4-5 years to recover, some tempo-rary, some permanent. As I weaned off my horrendous line-up of drugs, I became aware that not all was well with me. I was constantly falling over and breaking something, for which someone made fun of me. I was called an embarrassment continuously, clumsy klutz. I felt sad and alone, so the hiding intensified. I stopped going out on simple day-to-day trips. If I went anywhere, I ensured I was alone and shopped where no one else did. If I fell, it didn't matter; the chances were the falls wouldn't get back to Jesse. I broke many bones and injuries, so I had to find out what was causing it. I had been diagnosed with Migraine Associated Vertigo (MAV). I would never have guessed I had a migraine condition as I didn't have hangovers. I think my headaches were caused by sustained stress and the mental games that were inflicted on me.

To this day, I still have a shopping list of conditions weakening and degenerative.

I was medically evacuated from Germany in January 2011; I was gutted but in such a medical state. I cannot begin to tell you how relieved I was to be going back to Selly Oak for some running repairs to the injuries. I also was devastated I couldn't walk out of the Divisional HQ a proud person. Jesse fought hard with the MOD and German hospital, and I ended up having to give evidence in court. It was a horrendous experience; I had to relive it all over again. I had flashbacks, sweats and nightmares, and I couldn't escape any of them. Nine years later and I am still suffering from some of the injuries.

I returned to the UK, and being apart from the military family environ-ment in Germany was amazing. Having to leave Germany devastated me, but my injuries needed to be corrected. For me to return to work, I knew I would have had to have these corrective procedures. I did adjust, slowly but surely, and dreamt about what might have been.

I can remember that every day within the household was a warzone. Jesse somehow made it his mission to bring the Army down for what they had done to me. To be honest, it was more the fact he thought it was his meal ticket to a lot of money, should I have won my case. But the thing is, it wasn't my case; it was Jesse's war!

It seemed to the outside world that Jesse was this incredible fighter, an awesome person fighting for his wife's rights. But behind closed doors, this was far from the truth. Every conversation was negative and aggravated by temper tantrums and outbursts. Lengthy shouting, phone calls, threats, intimidation, all going on around me and directed at me whilst I recovered from operation after operation. I was then at my breaking point of sanity. I was freefalling from a plane, looking down on all the crap below me. I used to cringe and hide at all the above going on. I hated my home life when there was all this chaos around me and the girls.

Somehow Mr Fixit, surgeon No. 9, got me back to work slowly. It was an uphill fight but, after 18 months of being out of work with the MOD, I was back. Not the same, as there were bits of me broken, but I got back to the top of the mountain. Tough and long hours of being tortured seem as if it all were to get me flowing in the right direction. I do believe I was heading in the right direction but kept being dragged differently. I wasn't the best swimmer in the world. Never mind, try to get out of the deep end with lead weights attached. The lead weights were issues and things that bogged me down. I couldn't hold my breath underwater any longer; I was drowning until I met Paula. What a girl!

Paula was a woman whose daughter went to the same nursery as Lexie. She also worked in the MOD as a civil servant. I met her in the workplace first, and then for some reason, we bumped into each other at the nursery on the same day. From then onwards, we became friends. So, I now had a great friend called Gavin in the Blue corner and, in the Red corner, I had Paula. The downside is that Gavin thought Jesse was a good friend and fun to be around; on the other hand, Paula gave him shit. She wasn't that keen on him.

Innocently, she would pop round for a cuppa and bump into him and detested how he spoke and treated me. Paula hated Jesse but, for my sake, kept some comments to herself. Excellent for 13 years; we held each other up when times brought us down.

Chapter Eleven

Have you noticed one topic I haven't mentioned in this is Sex! I am struggling to bring it to the top, partly because of severe shame, disgust, and humiliation. I believe this is because I want to crawl under the stones and hide at my part in all this too. I haven't always been very forthcoming in this department; the phrase 'a bit of a prude' comes to mind.

When Jesse and I first started having a sex life, it was average and standard. It's not as if I had much previous experience to gauge it against, but it was ok; let's just say no issues that I remember. But sadly, yes indeed, this wasn't always the case. Not sure what happened, though. Part of me is confused, and a massive amount of me is in denial and doesn't want to believe what I want to reveal.

I have a fantastic counsellor, but I didn't get to declare all my heart after all these weeks together. I hate that side of me; chatty, yet I can hide and be secretive. I have been laughed at and belittled too many times. On occasion, from this day forward, I understand very clearly that things in the bedroom were going astray.

In the earlier days of our relationship, Jesse was a well-stocked guy. He weighed about 20 stone, but he didn't look huge around the tummy region because he was tall. He did have huge solid legs and arms; his mind was even more powerful, persuasive and overbearing.

These early days were what I felt to be as good ones for him and me, because this would be what I understand now to sound sick. I hear my counsellor trying to get me to "break it down." What's there to break down? Pain, heartache, terrible memories, shaking, fear, the list goes on.

One thing is for sure it's all genuine for me, but I can't look at myself in the mirror and reveal it all. It would be best for me if it all came out. I would be able to move on from it, I guess.

He would lay on top of me. I couldn't breathe, so I had weaknesses in my chest. Until he had finished, I couldn't move as I would be restrained, but it was getting more and more restrictive. His weight was physically weighing me down; he was like a roll-on-roll-off ferry. It used to leave me feeling cheap, sick; I can't even bring myself to say words anymore.

I can't remember an exact incident where you could outline a trigger or increase in behaviours; I can only remember I'm trying to block it all out. Over time I noticed I was more restricted, or should I say restrained. I don't remember having a voice or an option. Even if I didn't want anything to happen and spoke out, I was verbally and physically pushed into situations. Being told I had to show how grateful I was because "I saved your life; you need to be grateful" was being banished around.

When Jesse was drunk, or should I say when he had some drinks, he was more forceful. I'm not sure if I can take you on this same journey, but Jesse's weight became a ton when I got the severely injured right lung injury. He became more powerful when my lung had issues. I'm not sure if you can imagine the pain my chest used to have in these circumstances. That brought on fear, real fear, sudden coldness. Visualise being in some wood late on a winter's night and you're faced with a massive bear in front of you. That was me; I was in this unknown wood faced with that bear. There are no words in my speech to explain anymore. It became a daze and a blur, then pushed to the rear of my brain to try and make me forget. The forceful bedroom stuff haunts me still to this day – I am single with terrible flashbacks.

On many occasions, I was strangled to the point of nearly passing out. Yet I can't remember how I got to the bed. Why can't I recollect my steps? How did I end up not being able to breathe? I also remember nearly passing out, and when I gathered myself afterwards, I felt disgusted, sick; why did I feel like this? So, on one occasion, I asked what I was feeling, and all I got back was a load of abuse.

"You're f@@@ing sick in the head. We are husband and wife - you're a stupid bitch."

I was dazed and in shock. This happened; I hadn't imagined it.

"I'm only doing what husband and wife do."

I went downstairs and stared at the blank TV screen in a daze, shivering, fearful, yet honest. It had happened but still not finding the words; you don't want to believe it has happened. How do you tell people that? Who would believe you when this is a powerful person who is a sweet as honey in public and has another side behind closed doors? Well-known in the public circle, who would believe my version over his? In the Blue corner me, in the Red, him. Who do you believe? I knew that some sexual activity took place on these days, but I can only remember because I was wet downstairs with his smell. OMG, I feel sick; let's leave it here. Let's just put it back away in a tightly locked box and throw away the key.

I started to wear scarves around my neck to hide marks, wore trousers a lot, no one knew, the actress in me came out. I ask myself repeatedly why I kept it all so quiet. I simply thought that I was misreading and imagining all these sequences, and if anyone reads this, they will or have been the same. But this is what they programme us to do; they make us and shape us to think incorrectly. They, for want of a better word, install the virus and ensure it runs around in your system.

For the record, Paula was getting to see them, as on spa days, I would have faint marks on my neck, midriff and at the top of my legs. I would be quiet. I would not look in the direction of the discussions. She would reduce me to tears talking it through- Rather, I should say, she would state what it was; I just stayed silent and hopefully nodded in the right place. She always asked when? I never knew when - I couldn't remember how!

I would be marked for around 4-5 days before my injuries would go from the bright purple-blue to green, then yellow, fading. The trouble is that this happened to me more than I let on; I never spoke in public; I was silent, numb, dazed but still fighting my feelings and emotions. The fear, the touching, grabbing, roughness, the flashbacks never went away; they just replayed like the typical LP records.

I remember the needles on the LP going up, down and repeatedly round. For me, I was that LP. I couldn't wait for it all to play out and stop. Take the needle off me; I beg you, please stop playing the LP. If I didn't have children, I'm not sure where I would have ended up. One thing is for sure I stayed silent in the house throughout these episodes because I had children in the home, waifs, strays, and Lexie. The day after these sessions, I would be withdrawn; I didn't engage in conversation, I appeared moody. I would get a rollicking for being like this the following day. I would try and explain but be shut down in seconds. I wanted to tell someone, but the LP in me forbade me to move, speak or seek help. I was frozen in time. Strangled in the bed, was it really what a husband does to his wife?

I was highly fortunate later in my life as Jesse had a slight drinking problem on any normal day. One thing that started to happen was that he struggled with any length of time to keep it stiff. What had previously been four minutes of an episode was soon becoming two mins or less. I know it's a sick way of explaining it, but I hope you understand where my mind was and how I learnt to deal with it. I knew some of the dangers of these incidences.

I've spoken to Gavin and his wife Bonnie today, and it's always lovely to hear their voices, but more importantly, as I write this, I feel I wish I were closer. Sometimes I don't allow myself to really love them; this is because I know someone in my life that doesn't want me to have any friends. In fact, Jesse doesn't want me to have anything. Which could be a thing, a person; he wants me to be naked. Jesse makes me constantly feel he wants me dead.

I love Gavin dearly, not because I am attracted to him because I aspire to deal with things how he does. He is an Eifel Tower of a person: a person mountain, paired up with a wee Scottish girl that blows your mind. I am blessed to have them guide me through life when the doors are shut. More importantly, they both equally get me; I make a mess of things, and they help me see that there are other ways to have addressed it. I wish Gavin were happier, though, as he sometimes seems sad; leaving the Army, you say goodbye to your family. The fluffy blanket is no longer underneath your feet to keep you safe; it's nowhere to be seen. You stood alone for that split second, but I realised what I had when someone destroyed it for me. It would devastate me if they were got at like some of my friends.

I wish I had something to make Gavin have fire in his belly, but I also hope to take all his bad memories away. At the same time, I feel I need to do this for myself too. I have always tried to give everything to everyone that has now left me alone and exhausted. Today I am totally knackered; I look drained and don't feel so great. The stress of living a life I don't like. But I am working with my counsellor and friends to chip away at the layers I have built around me that made me detest everything about myself.

Drinking was one vice that never went away, nor did it subside.

One night, Jesse came home bladdered in the night, and he peed in the chest of drawers. I was, to say the least, annoyed because it was my chest of drawers, not his.

I got up early in the morning, brought a scrubbing brush bowl of hot soapy water, and awoke the bear to clean it all up. He had no idea or memory he had done it. The funny thing is that Lexie was out of nappies; I should have put him in them. His wee was on the carpet and all in the drawers. I was appalled that Lexie witnessed her daddy scrubbing his mess up. Lexie asked him what he was doing, and he said making the carpet nice and clean. Lexie asked why, but he shouted at her to go away; he was so aggressive. She came to ask me why dad was scrubbing the carpet. I replied that daddy had forgotten where the toilet was and had urinated in the drawers and carpet by mistake. I couldn't lie to her; she had made comments on the smell. I just couldn't think on my feet what to say to her, other than the sort of truth.

His temper the morning after drinking binges was scary, but I did my best to keep the girls safer than myself. It was best to duck and dive, avoid conflict, try to ignore his actions, behaviours, comments. I also hated coming home if I knew he was there. I am unsure what that is all about, but I was clearly frightened of something.

Chapter Twelve

A horrific event happened whilst we were away in Tenerife on Boxing Day 2015; I got a call from Alexa to say Lucille's daughter, my granddaughter, Poppy, had died. It wasn't as if I could drop to the floor; emotionally, I knew something was up when Alexa called out of the blue. Dread, horrendous, where do you even start to comprehend this tragedy?

A 12-week-old baby girl dies: you're abroad, you're broken. I wasn't there for Lucille; I was on the other side of the world. I also couldn't get to speak with Lucille at that time. I sent texts to let her know I would get home - somehow. My ex-husband kept in touch. To this day, I do not understand how she died. All I do know is it's safe to say she possibly died of Sudden Infant Death Syndrome (cot death). The place she died has two versions of events. From that day forward, I have constantly struggled with Christmas, especially Boxing Day.

I can't talk about this anymore; all I can say is that Paula came with me to the graveside, not Jesse. He had long gone emotionally and physically. That was the turning point when I knew my marriage was wrong. The reason I stayed – the girls, my invested efforts, my lifetime of climbing to get where I wanted to get in life. How can your husband show not one ounce of understanding when your granddaughter dies and be there for you…?

My life, alone, isolated. You always believe you'll go before your children, never mind your grandchildren. I felt sick to the stomach, thinking of what Lucille must have been going through. She struggled. I just can't comprehend her feelings, her emotions, how she coped. All

I can say is that I am so goddamn proud of her. All I can say about Jesse is what a scumbag he was. I miss my Granddaughter every day; it never dies or decreases; it's just walking away from my reach. I can't hold on to it forever. It's a tragic event that I didn't physically cause, but it is one I wish I could change.

My whole life has been blighted by death and misfortune that make up horrible memories. Worse was to come, though, so now I need to refocus on what I want to say to help prevent someone else from making my mistakes. The writing was on the wall; I just didn't see the invisible ink until it was gone over in a permanent black marker.

Never in my life did it enter my head that I would be around to bury two children in less than a year; Stephen was 12 and suffered from painful asthma. Mama A was Lexie's childminder. She was African Caribbean and was amazingly good with her son Stephen's ill health. He would get into awful breathing problems; he then banged on his radiator, and Mama A would go running upstairs to help. In an emergency, it was a 999 job, but the rest of the time, Mama A was there.

One day he didn't bang on the radiator; it was too bad and too late. It was desperately sad because the father just took to drink and wasn't even allowed to attend the funeral for Stephen. A beautiful boy has gone way too soon.

In 2016 we all moved into a fresh start. It was sold to Lexie and me that we would have this huge house with everything we needed and more. It was also told to Lexie that Daddy darling wanted to buy her a pony! We were so obviously, being hoodwinked, robbed, and denied of reality. It was nothing like what had been outlined. Jesse's a salesman and a crook at best. The house was enormous, but with my wages and his, it was affordable. I had reservations, but every avenue was clearly resolved without me. Jesse had everything planned right down to the acceptance letter.

Countryside location, what I had always dreamed of, not overlooked, needed some work - all the ticks. For Lexie, the countryside would be easy to find locations for a pony, great schools, a bigger bedroom, and it ticked all she needed. As for Jesse, I now, years later, realise what it was all about…. sauna, man cave, Jacuzzi, huge house, massive garden.

The home was stunning, but I always felt something was wrong, and it ended up I was right. The garden flooded every winter, the plasterwork was awful, it was expensive to keep warm. I got stuck in decorating, planning for the wood supplies, cutting down trees to prepare for seasons one, two and three of wood for the open fire. In every moment of spare time, I worked on the house and dealt with Lexie's needs, taking her to school on my way to work and all her sporting trips.

I also took Lexie horse riding every weekend and sometimes during the week. Looking back, I was one heck of a busy lady but it was because I was managing everything independently. I was a single mother, slave, cook, cleaner, worker, DIY person; I had every skill set going; what I wasn't was a partnership. Although Jesse worked, he did the square root of nothing around the house or with Lexie. Well, with anything other than if it was all about him.

His boasting about what a large house he had became a constant issue. Sadly, it increased and continued, so what was supposed to have been a new start was right, but it wasn't what it was first outlined to be.

The fresh start soon became horrific torture, nightmare after nightmare, flashbacks, fear. I was in totally over my head; I mean, the depths were like the sea; you can only go so far down before your drowning. As I said earlier, I am not the best swimmer. Clearly, I was better than I thought at times, and I stayed the rest of the time afloat. I was pushed so far under that I am surprised I am still here. I hear the song 'I Will Survive' and, although I always thought it was about a broken marriage, it could be interpreted to be about life in any circumstances. It relates to my life like Velcro sticks to fabric.

On occasions, I would pass Jesse on the landing, but what started as an innocent manoeuvre soon became a place where I was terrified. Over the years, it was a minor incident when I would be in the vicinity of the top of the stairs. I had walked out of the bathroom with just a bath sheet wrapped around me. He would shove his face right in mine, in a threatening and intimidating manner. When I passed a comment about it, he would come at me more and more. I quickly just learnt to ensure I was not there when he was. I soon started witnessing him doing this to his petite child; she then was becoming his target.

Lexie eventually left the private school, and I enrolled her into an excellent school located in the village. It was a dumb deal as in I had arranged everything for her. The only reason for such a change in her schooling came about from the fact that I had seen and heard enough. I will try and convert what I mean by that into reality without the emotional drive that clearly lay underneath it all.

There was immense pressure on Lexie attending a grammar school via the evil Smother-in-Law, piling the heaps of burden onto her.

Lexie is Lexie; she's a funny character who, if she can walk away and say, "I tried my best, Mum," I'm a happy mummy. This would absolutely pee everyone else off around her. I mean the immense pressure of Lexie being a genius - she must take or be seen that every test she took was like her life depended on it. She had to be the cleverest at the school, and if she wasn't, the criticism became an onslaught for her. But don't worry, I was there for her, verbally and emotionally I wasn't just going to listen to it all and do nothing. Lexie found some subjects a little more complicated than others, but she was bright and took it on board eventually. Let's be honest there is no rush into how you are educated, is there? Who cares which school avenue you go down?

I saw Lexie doing her best, and I hope she noticed I supported her; she knew I would fight for her. My lovely, delightful Smother-in-Law saw things differently. Lexie was being told off all the time about her educational standard and was never allowed or encouraged to have an opinion on anything.

Behind my back, they wanted Lexie to stay with them all the school holidays (every day). Again, the Smother-in-Law was going to get many test papers. The outlined expectation was that Lexie would sit there being pressured into doing at least four test papers every day throughout the seven-week summer holiday. It was a dumb deal; Lexie didn't have a voice, nor was she considered. Indeed, she should have a right to a view and asked if this was what she wanted. The walls were closing in on her, so I intervened and said that Lexie would have a private tutor to assess her to see if it was worthwhile to do the grammar school exams.

I had no evidence that a) this was what Lexie wanted b) just pressure, lots of money, etc. It was always stated that since Lexie was born, she would be driven into the grammar school route. Because the Smother-in-Law and sister-in-law Maud had both been down these routes, it was stated that Lexie couldn't let them all down. As time goes on, a mother knows a child's capability, so I tried to fend her off and thought I should get an expert to see if she could do the exams.

It's a rat race, isn't it? Your children are pushed through a process because you think you're doing the right thing for them. But it's all about what you can brag and boast about. I knew somehow that this wasn't the route for Lexie; however, I needed the confidence to speak out and defend her. Basically, shut everyone up and get them to back off her.

So, I found a team to assess Lexie academically, and they stated that Lexie was an excellent student, but she would struggle with the test and competition standards. The results cemented the idea that Lexie should not be forced into the grammar school option as her only route of schooling. I understood at the time that 1270 children had passed the exam, but only 135 places were offered. I know all about the pressure to be something you're not, but this was a primary school child who hadn't been a straight-A student across-the-board, but she was a great, consistent student.

Lexie received 'lovely to teach' comments the whole time she attended military and private schools, so leaving this environment to attend a great school like Henley-in-Arden was a little difficult. This school was on par with Lexie's background of schools. In my eyes, I saw Lexie being bullied, and it seemed like only I wanted her to be safe. There is no shame in not attending the grammar school environment, but I guess it stops people from boasting – portraying your life is something it's not. I wanted Lexie to be Lexie without the constant negative comments. She developed becoming sick and the runs when it was exam time… I wonder how that happened? The continuous comparisons were like a dam bursting its bridges, flooding and overwhelming.

Throughout all of Lexie's primary age, I don't ever recall her dad being proud of her. I remember terrible memories of him sitting, looking at his mobile with his glasses on his forehead, not supporting his daughter. I remember losing my rag with them all to make them realise what they were saying to Lexie. She's a child but also their granddaughter and daughter, but don't worry, I had plenty to say in the car on the way home! I thought grandparents were there to support and nurture their own flesh and blood. Clearly, it was just down to me to protect Lexie and myself at this point in my life. By god, it was a lonely phase when you're made out to be the troublemaker, and they deemed their comments to be totally acceptable. I would always disagree. But was I right or wrong to defend her?

Lexie met Charlotte at her new school and soon settled in; it was as if she was comfortable with her surroundings and school process. Charlotte had the exact same interests as Lexie, and they soon became great friends and inseparable. A friendship that even to this day has not deteriorated despite someone's best attempts to sabotage it. They both rode; they were both loud, one thought it, and the other said it.

Going through school can be challenging, but having a genuine and trustworthy friend can make school life a lot easier.

Chapter Thirteen

Lexie has been horse riding since she was three years old; she first sat on a horse at my mum and dad's some months beforehand. Lexie was taught in Germany riding Smartie; she was hilarious trying to do a riding trot. She once got thrown off on a bend, well she was so tiny and lightweight I am not sure he even knew she was there. The pony just decided for some unknown reason to ditch her, and she got straight up, walked to the front of the pony, and started shouting at him.

She said, "I was nice to you – why did you do that to me?"

Just imagine seeing the daintiest of little girls, wagging her finger in the horse's face. Then she threw her tiny leg out and asked for a leg back up, to which the military guy teaching her couldn't contain his laughter.

Lexie rode out in minus 28ºC; she was very willing and loved to go. She would have her pink clothes to go riding with a red coat, hat and body protector.

Now, 11 years on, she still is an avid horse rider, but no pink clothes, thank goodness. She's talented and educated in horses, and when she needs to seek advice, she calls my mum (the font of all knowledge).

When we returned from Germany, I looked for a horse riding coach on the internet and found Margaret Bees, who just happened to be in the top ten dressage riders and had a helicopter. Initially, Lexie was around 6/7 years old, and Mrs Bees said she didn't take children that young to ride. However, Lexie really wanted to learn the trade and Mrs Bees started to include Lexie more by introducing her to horses.

When she introduced a horse that she wanted Lexie to look at,

Lexie asked why. Mrs Bees told her that the horse had just come from Germany, and she was having issues with it. So there again is this tiny framed young girl oozing with confidence who spoke to the horse in German. The horse responded and snuggled into Lexie straight away; she totally blew Mrs Bees away with her immediate shock and surprise.

I was always a taxi service for Lexie. I watched her with immense pride, and still to this day, nine years on, I'm still doing it. It never ceases to get boring. Lexie did some competitions and was successful. I paid for all her safety equipment and lessons to ensure she got the best of the experiences on offer.

Mind you, one thing that I can't explain is why for these four years, I have no idea why her father didn't support or watch her every time. In fact, it was something that he didn't show any interest in, other than trying to stop her from doing what appeared to be what she loved and woke up for every day.

Lexie was becoming a much better rider when she wanted to ride faster, so I found a junior jockey riding course over in Newmarket for her to attend. She was placed on the system with children older than her and no famous relatives to name drop. She was the youngest by five years, plus the lightest and smallest, but she was one of the few who managed to stay on her horse throughout the assessments. Lexie absolutely loved it. She slept all the way home, but you could just tell she got a buzz from it all.

Her inherited passion for riding led her onto further adventures that became a lot more exciting and challenging for her further down this road. I will hopefully remember to come back to this. I think you can start seeing that Lexie and my diaries were becoming very full. The more time we spent with the horses meant the less time she and I spent at home. If I think back, this was clearly what was happening. Avoidance, filling our time in to ensure the least amount of time was spent in that house. God, why didn't I see that as what it was at the time?

Despite having this magnificent property in Warwickshire, which Jesse wanted, and ideas sold to Lexie and me in a way that looking back was totally blindfolded. You'll understand why in a bit. With this fantastic village school, developing awesome friendships, it was a lot to take on board. The house was so blooming big, décor was old fashioned, but that was just a lick of paint and some alterations.

Jesse suggested that we were financially secure, and we could afford for me to take my foot off the gas. He wanted to keep me. Is that how you say it?

"I want to look after you; you don't need to work, darling."

So eventually, with my medical condition worsening, he persuaded me to give in. He was right in one way that the medical people were struggling to stabilise my situation, so it slightly made sense. Well, it would do, wouldn't it? The idea and concept of me relaxing after over 30 years of working. Being told I would be financially protected and reassured of this. Yeah, that was this silly cow writing this now.

All it was, it's becoming logical, looking back, was another way to stop me from being seen out, for me to be in to get his parcels from Amazon and God knows what else. Food shopping deliveries would come at stupid o'clock. Meaning I was becoming tied to the house; he always knew where I was at any one time. God forbid I went out and didn't answer my phone. I would be punished by either silence for 8-9 days or with a massive argument. This further dictated that the result would be three weeks of subjected silence; either way meant the same thing.

The silence became a killer for me, but you guessed right, it was a pre-plan of his all along. What it meant was that he would go upstairs and be secretly texting and speaking to someone. When I asked who he was chatting to, he denied he'd spoken to anyone and said I needed help.

"It's all in your f@@@@@@ head."

What I can never accept is that I hadn't imagined it at all, nor had I made it up. It was so real to me I cannot even put it into any further descriptions. I believe he was unfaithful for most of our relationship. I have some clear evidence, and some is a little shady. I do know one thing - there was a reason I felt like I did, and no matter how much the pressure built, it needed to be shut down. These feelings would not go away and kept coming up. It was never going to happen. It was real. It wasn't my imagination.

We kept the car keys in a cupboard, so every night, I would place my keys away in there. Spare keys for sheds, doors, cars were all in one place. One day I was going out and had to be there on time. I went to get the keys from the cupboard, but nope… they weren't there. Panic was stepping in, and I was becoming late. He was working at the house, but clearly not because it later turned out that he moved all the keys to make out that I could not be responsible for keys.

It was another thing Jesse could take control of me on. Little did I know it was a deliberate act to ensure I didn't go to my appointment. The keys were all put back hours later after my panic-stricken run around the house, retracing my steps. Jesse went straight to them in the cupboard, and the name-calling commenced again. I soon learnt to always keep my keys with me. What a way to live or exist? A game for one person where they mentally play with you soon becomes a fearful element that is being forced upon you and your inability to stop it.

As time went on, Jesse would come home to the immaculate house, and the enormous garden was spotless. I was repeatedly told how every room was decorated to a high standard. Lexie was attended to, so what I am trying to say is that there was nothing for Jesse to do. Over a period, Jesse would sit in his living room secretly doing stuff on his phone, and I would sit in mine, separated. Lexie was with me in our living room as it became known; only we sat in it.

In April 2018, there was a serious incident between Lexie and her dad. Serious because it was verbally violent. Let me wind back to ensure you understand where I am coming from.

Jesse and I had been relaxing about our issues, and I had always wanted to be a foster mum. I was already looking after the Chinese boys, so it really would be the next step. However, I never thought it was meant to be because I felt I would never be good enough. Not realising all the seriousness of my relationship with Jesse, not acknowledging what was happening.

As I proceeded to apply to be a foster mum, Jesse was counting the pennies before I could get the application form over the line. We did attend the start of the courses. Shocked and like a fish out of water, inappropriate comments; this was a serious issue. I wanted this for most of my life, yet it was being ruined before it took off. Part of the process is what I would perceive to be intense questioning. Lexie was very level-headed and grown-up, helpful and supportive. She was looking forward to having a child between the ages of 8-14ish in the house with her.

Something still happening was the rabbit punches and evil gestures. So, if I smiled, I got a thump on my damaged arm. Triggering the CRPS Type II was nothing new, so I learnt to retract going into his spaces. This would limit these opportunities of him hitting or verbally screaming at me.

But I've had to come back to this space to let you know about a knife incident. Despite 1000's of incidences, some serious and some minor, I felt I was running a mental marathon every day that some issues haven't come out yet.

Jesse was in the kitchen sharpening knives whilst allegedly working from the house. My friend turned up for a cuppa; she wasn't frightened of him at all. She saw through Jesse; she could handle his comments, and her comments were intelligent responses that shut him up. When Jesse was revering up and kicking, you knew to hide and be quiet. Innocently, I greeted her and asked if she wanted a cuppa.

She replied, "Yes, please."

So, a cuppa it is.

I walked into the kitchen, and Jesse was sharpening our knives. He asked what the hell I was doing; I responded I was making a cuppa. With that, Jesse went from 0 to 100 in a millisecond in a complete rage. I quickly previously learnt to ensure I always had an escape plan. If I was feeling scared of him, I knew where to go to get away from him. His sharpening technique began to be coming towards me fiercely and intently. I walked back towards the large lounge with three exits.

In this entire episode of temper, he totally forgot that my friend was sitting in the lounge, witnessing what I had been trying to hide from everyone. All this temper outburst was because I went into the kitchen within this massive countryside property to make a cuppa. It left me thinking deeply about what would have happened to me had no one else been in the house. Would he have taken my life as his temper was so out of control? It just seemed to go that bit further.

I would be walking across the landing after coming out of the bathroom. An innocent, normal event, yet if Jesse greeted you, he would back you up to the top of the stairs and scare you. Just enough to make you think you could fall backwards.

What did I do so wrong to deserve the threatening and intimating manner? I seem to be ok with giving you information about anything but not everything. But I want you to know that it doesn't take a lot to think it's your fault. You're mentally worn down, physically shattered, your body is bruised. Your head is totally battered, and you're trying to keep your guard up, but you doubt everything about anything.

As Christmas came and went, thank bloody goodness. It was becoming undeniable that he was kicking off that I wasn't at work anymore. Hang on a minute; it took Jesse months to persuade me to throw the towel in and concede. You convinced me to give up work after over 33 years of professional background. You explicitly stated you wanted to look after Lexie and me financially, and you didn't want me working. This was clearly a planned attack to ensure I had nothing. Jesse owned everything, despite all the years I had worked and was still working, just not getting paid for it.

Jesse worked on me as he always did to persuade me to have Airbnb. I was nervous at the start because of Lexie, but he then wanted the other rooms rented out with Students after that. As I was at home, it would be good for me to bring in some money. So, one minute you want me to do all the jobs all the time before you get home? Now you want me to work my socks off despite my medical conditions spiralling? Not at any point did he ever collect Lexie from school and attend all the parent's evenings (Jesse missed countless ones). Now I had a house guest and a Student to run around after on top of his expectations of the daily chores. It was him that came in, got changed and went straight out. Do you know why? He was earning; it gave him that right he would state.

I refused to go out with him on most occasions, and people were becoming aware that I didn't exist, nor did Lexie in his life. When he went out, he would think he's funny and clever with his mouth, but it's cringeworthy when you are with him. I used to hide at first in Warwickshire, not because I had done anything wrong, but because I was ashamed of his behaviour. To this day, I am convinced he was deliberately setting me up to argue back (defend myself), so it gave him the right to be free to go out without a care in the world.

Imagine your daughter, who was about 10/11 years old, going to some beautiful riding stables and her dad not even taking her five miles down the road. Or, in one case, she was less than a mile and a half away, and he still didn't go to watch her. Lexie, at times, was craving to gain her dad's attention but only got slaps around the head, her hair or ears pulled.

I don't think Jesse could go an hour without winding a child up then standing back with his hands held up, saying to the parent, your child's out of control, mate! I had witnessed him poking fun, teasing, name-calling these children until they retaliated back.

I used to get myself in all sorts of trouble defending Maud's son, Jacob Harold. He was a ginger-haired lad that was subjected to drinking milk all the time. He didn't have a voice; everyone spoke around him, and he only communicated when asked. He was silenced; his teeth needed braces as most children's teeth do; however, Jesse just constantly scolded Jacob Harold. I mean, it was an onslaught of abuse. I can't lie; it brought out the worst in me defending Jacob Harold. That red mist would begin to fall towards their attitudes. The Smother-in-Law and Jesse thought it was funny to humiliate this young lad who was a nephew and a grandson. What was wrong with these folks?

Chapter Fourteen

In September 2017, Jesse was diagnosed with pancreatitis, brought on by his constant drinking; he's a diabetic too.

When he was in the hospital, you'd have thought this was a one-off health incident, and everyone should help him now. Well, the truth of the matter was that he'd caused this all himself. I brought in food and his clothes, but on one occasion, he was vile, and a patient over the other side of the ward spoke out about his behaviour towards me. He screamed back at this bloke, and he took control of verbally battering this poor guy. I left him there and wouldn't go to see him until he had apologised. Don't worry, that didn't happen; he couldn't say sorry.

I need to rewind to give you a more precise run-up to what happened. We had all been on holiday to Portugal. Jesse's best mate Malc lived out there; his wife had died, so we all went to see him. Dana was a heck of a girl; she died too young, riddled with rare cancer.

Malc had been in my life since 2002. I haven't mentioned him before, but a) there is so much that I could say about this amazing person, b) the whole picture will be revealed later. I think Malc got me as in understood me. I loved the bones of him; he was someone I looked up to.

I had gone on this holiday as a nanny. Why am I saying this? It's because I was just there to play my part in making up the numbers. I have always jokingly said to people that Lexie and I were just a front for Jesse to get his inheritance. How accurate was this becoming? I used to say to people he's gay - I'm convinced... It was worrying to see the lad's holiday, play out scene by scene in slow motion. That's a good way of saying how it really was looking back.

I went on holiday to see Malc because we had a great relationship, laughed, and joked, genuinely got on. We had similar interests, but I also held him when he was despondent about Dana passing. The whole holiday Jesse and Malc would get totally plastered like a pair of teenagers. I was left with Lexie all the time; I was also abandoned, but I didn't mind because Jesse was out of my hair. I used to feel I couldn't cope without him by my side, but guess what? I was starting to install some scaffolding into my backbone. I could take Lexie to the beach; I could cook, I could be on my own, I could find some peace.

I was mentally picked back up and only spoken to on the following day. He was out drinking at 1pm, he'd come back, I would be acknowledged, and then it would all start over again at night. I did all the shopping, cooking, and cleaning, babysit Lexie. I also learnt from about day two to just do my own thing with Lexie on the beach, play with her, keep her entertained, etc. I love spending time with any of my children. I also had my own set of house keys to Malc's apartment. Don't get me wrong, Malc loved me looking after him, but I couldn't always take Lexie to the beach. The weather was severe for redheads, so it was a bikini for her and a t-shirt over the top.

Malc took us to several places off the beaten track to show us Portugal. Lexie and I made Jesse look normal, but Malc was always so natural with Lexie. Even if I glance at these older photos, you can see a genuine love for her. Malc should have been what I had wanted for Lexie, not what I had got. Don't be disillusioned. Malc was a drinker, but his behaviours didn't change – no violence, no rudeness, it was just funny watching him moving around and stuff. What a bloke he is, or is he?

Malc was particularly good to Lexie and me. I also understood that Malc, as much as he loved Jesse, had an unusual relationship. I think it was a set-up from the outset. I will never forget the looks between Lexie and Malc; every time, it won me over. So where is he now? Blooming good question. Another friend, missing from the action.

Malc didn't always speak with high regard for Jesse; in fact, although they got on, Malc would not hesitate to freely open his unfiltered mouth, and he got away with it. You're right: he did get away with it, but neither Lexie nor I did. The backlash was mine to own unless Jesse got to Lexie before me. It came to a point I stopped entrusting Jesse with Lexie on his own; if he took Lexie somewhere, I ensured I went too. I just couldn't leave her to be picked apart bit by bit. What a way of life that you couldn't trust that the biological father would provide a safe and loving environment. It seems I knew it wasn't going to end well.

All the slagging off statements, such as, "You're mental. It's all in your head!" are constantly thrown at you. It leaves the best of people doubting your own minds. But it wasn't my mind that was in danger of caving in; it was my soul and heart.

I think I must have become protective over Lexie; she needed one parent to love and care for her the right way. She also needed one of us to step up and show her right from wrong. I can't write much about what happened to Lexie because, at some point, she will read this and Pandora's box will open. I would like to sit her down when she's ready to talk about it. Because she was a child when we escaped, she's forgotten what happened to her. It's fair to say much the same as me; the rabbit punches to your body as he passes, the name-calling, physical violence, threats, the innocent visits to a friend and he comes to snatch her away against her will. A giant mug of tea in one hand, driving dangerous country roads at high speeds, the list goes on.

So, for example, in an argument, you didn't need to ultimately say something repulsive to the other person to get the upper hand. You didn't need to start a verbal discussion over the jam jar because you wanted to go out for the night and not come back.

Yes, I had worked all this out over the years; this is possible when lying about where Jesse would be. Don't get me wrong, part of me did not care, but I thought it should have been so different with a child. Why wouldn't he want to spend his time with a beautiful home life…and a gorgeous daughter who he should have loved? Something wasn't right.

Lexie suffered in so many ways that I was there for her without her even knowing. Lexie was expected to attend private school and be a fantastic student - an excellent A grade, nothing else would do. Lexie was the only granddaughter; therefore, she had an enormous part to play in the family. But in Lexie's own way, I could see her struggling slightly with one or two things. They started off small, but I was young once, and I could see it in her eyes. Her eyes have a way of telling you something, which we are supposed to do for our children.

Life was drifting, sinking, violent, sick, abused, emotionally battered, raped and bruised, but I was piecing it together that things were very wrong. It took me a long time to describe what was happening to me. Domestic Abuse, that's what! When you hear it for the first time, you freak out.

But I must be brutely honest and come back to a complete volcano that happened.

On a Tuesday after school, Lexie was due to be questioned by the Social Services for fostering for the final time. Ensuring she was fully content to have these strangers coming and going in the house, Lexie was nervous, but I reassured her that her answers must be hers. I advised her to answer slowly and clearly, and I am sure the Social Service lady would understand her. Devastatingly this is a copy of an email I had to issue:

It's taken me weeks to put down on here what I want to say without making it any worse than it already is.

Saturday was a horrendous day for you, me and Lexie, and nothing has been said today. I suppose everyone is just numb from what has happened.

Lexie has her conclusion interview with the social services tomorrow/Tuesday night. Considering you swore "F@@@ Off" yesterday directly to her in a heated argument, I believe this will end the fostering process. I don't want Lexie to lie to Catherine tomorrow/Tuesday. If she tells them what happened word for word, my fostering application is completely dead in the water.

We all play a part in life, but fostering was the one thing I have yearned about for decades; I thought I would be able to help a damaged child, recover and move forward with their life. However, we could never do that with Saturday's latest outburst.

I am totally horrified that you threw Lexie's card and stated you didn't want anything to do with her in front of her. You told her to F off straight her face; you were so close to her you were spitting at her. I tried to reason with you as it was your dad's birthday, and we never know how many more he has. When Lexie stormed off into the village without her phone, I also can't believe you said she would come back when she's cold and hungry. You proceeded to get into the car and go to your sisters. You just had a cold look which will haunt me for a long time. There was nothing in your eyes…

You've killed everything, you have stolen everything, but I will never understand why. Lexie was virtually the adult here and told Social Services how she didn't feel safe around you and didn't want another child to deal with that. She was so brave, so do not ever accuse her of it being the result of my decisions.

I feel totally devastated at all the hard work I have done to improve our family life and support you, which is all to no avail.

I have a duty of care to protect Lexie and our Chinese lads to provide a safe environment, and as it currently stands, this is certainly not the case. Since December 2016, I have tried to see if the situation will improve, and at times it does, but as soon as I relax, it all goes astray.

Therefore, this is what is going to happen:

1) You can leave the house voluntarily, and we will let the dust settle before we take any action.

2) I will get a court order to remove you from the house.

3) I move out with Lexie and seek family support payments from you – with immediate effect.

4) I will speak with Social Services and ensure the process stops – citing personal reasons to ensure I don't lose any face over this mess.

You lied about this house, and I have begged you for over twelve months to move; I've also begged you to sell one of the houses to free up some cash to help pay these huge repairs for this house. I don't want to be yours or anyone's prisoner. I have to say, Jesse, we are over, and if we are honest, we have been so toxic for a long time. I can't go on; I have nothing left to give you. I cannot let you do what you're doing to me anymore.

I really want you to listen to what I have written, which is written with a very heavy heart and lots of sadness after two decades. I am done with you.

Chapter Fifteen

Lexie proceeded to come home from school and make an excuse to go to one of my friend's. She saw this as her haven, I guess, someplace where there were no furious arguments or atmosphere. Most nights she would disappear on her bike, run to my friend's, or basically hide somewhere.

One day I innocently went to the bank, fifteen minutes tops. On my way back, an unknown number called my mobile it was a stranger saying she had found Lexie sopping wet. She was underneath a bridge in the village where there was water. I flew home to establish Jesse had again gone for her viciously. She couldn't cope with Jesse when he wasn't in a rage, never mind a full-blown tantrum. There wasn't a natural child and father relationship. What I witnessed was seeing her fear, disappointment, and constant shortfalls. Lexie wanted to be noticed, acknowledged, and loved but never got that. Unless money was thrown at her, she received nothing from Jesse. How sad is that? Approval, love, cuddles are all for free, yet Lexie received an empty vessel of a father.

Lexie went to my friend's one night to hide, or should I say, escape. She was having tea there; however, Jesse came home from work in a foul mood. He was gunning for a verbal fight, but I thought with Lexie out of the way, she would be safe. How stupid was I again? Years ago, he punished me by taking her from the nursery, and yes, Jesse did it again. He drove to where she was and continued to drive up and down a couple of hundred yards, wheel spinning gravel and pipping his horn. Lexie was furious and went out to his car. From what I understand, she had no choice other than to get into his car to shut him up. I understood she didn't want to, but she did. He drove very erratically and fast, which scared her.

When she returned to the house hours later, she was in such a state. He, of course, denied it all and made out Lexie was lying. My friend called me in such a panic, stating what had happened. I must admit that what I should have done was call the police. At this stage, I want you to know the thoughts had crossed my mind, but my fear made the decision.

I did some digging and found a Women's Refuge. I received some advice and found that I needed their help more than I chose to realise. Critical for me was the knowledge and little tricks they give you. I never thought I was a woman needing refuge specialist help. Let's be honest; we owed five properties, two of which were holiday cottage businesses. I thought this only happened to people who didn't own their own house. Silly and naïve, I didn't fit into this support network. But it was what I needed; you do realise nearer the time.

As time passed by, I secretly went to see many solicitors with what was happening, but again and again, people wouldn't take this case on. The main reason was that I was being financially controlled, which raised a serious issue of paying - somewhat a dealbreaker. I was getting desperate, and then my mum put me in touch with someone who said yes.

Naomi and Charlotte were now my legal team. Naomi was nice but incredibly quiet; I wondered if she believed what was happening but also, was she strong enough to deal with this monster? Charlotte became someone who was pinnacle on a particular day for calling 999 for me. I hated telling them anything about what was going on. That would mean I would be accepting what was happening around me.

When I was running for the hills, scared and threatened, I knew I would be running out of the town like all his other live-in girlfriends. I was threatened one day about all the houses and monies. I don't think people took it seriously; I was in such a mess. Frightened and alone, but I had Lexie to consider, first and foremost.

Bear in mind that Lexie and I just about survived an extra three months within the house. Also, this was since the above critical email was sent.

I've come back to this spot six months after I thought this book was ready to be published. I remembered, whilst driving, a huge flashback happened that I needed to come back to and slot in.

One day, I planned to go to Cumbria with Lexie to see some dearest of friends. So, the plan was to get on the train right outside our huge countryside property, with two small suitcases for Lexie and me. What happened was that when I wasn't looking, Jesse put the suitcases in his car and locked it. I became concerned he was holding us hostage and dependent on him taking us to our train, yet we could physically walk it in five minutes. Why was this happening? Well, the flashbacks driving along a country lane brought this all back to the forefront of my memory.

I ordered us all to get into the car, and he took us to another train station a few miles away. So, imagine driving at 60-70 on country lanes; Jesse with a 1-pint cup of tea in his right hand. Whilst thrashing his car at high speeds on single wide country lanes, I noticed that Lexie didn't have her rear seatbelt on. In a huge panic, she was being thrown around in the rear of his car and holding onto the edge of seats and the rear handles. It was the scariest car ride I had been in for a while, and with Jesse, I had somehow forgotten the trivial bits.

When we arrived at the train station, he virtually ran with our suitcases to the train platform. No acknowledgement for Lexie, no nothing. His eyes were dead, and by now, you know what that means.

Lexie and I had a great time up north; however, we returned to our dog being mysteriously crippled on the back end! All very strange. Lexie's riding crop had been removed from inside her wardrobe and found downstairs; I asked Lexie why this was. Then the penny dropped. I had severe concerns he beat the dog. The only thing that Lexie and I really loved and cared for. It is at least very suspicious what did happen to the dog that day I will never know the truth. But going along with all the actions of the train station incident, I can only think the worst. To this day, three years later, this young dog has injuries that cannot be explained.

Moving back to the real-time where we were still in the house - Jesse forced Lexie to go outside with him for a chat. She demonstrated she didn't want to go. I don't know what I mean about this, but I felt she would be mentally unsafe with him. I can't seem to describe it; maybe I tried to push it to the back of my brain too much to know what it meant. Jesse took Lexie to a bench at the far corner of our huge garden. Lexie faced away from her dad; Jessie had his arms and legs crossed with a stern face and angry lines. I could not hear what was being said, but I became aware that it wasn't good for her.

After about 20 minutes, Lexie dashed back into the house. She was screaming, saying she wasn't allowed to tell me what Jesse had said to her. She vented her anger, not making any sense at all. I couldn't leave it at this, so I followed her to the bedroom to ask if she was ok. God, she was in such an emotional mess, confused, screaming, not stringing a sentence together. Jesse went out the front door, closing it, or should I say slamming it; he drove off at speed. Lexie was confused, so I cuddled her and asked if she wanted to talk about it. Maybe I should have written it down, but I didn't need to. Lexie was speaking quite clearly under the circumstances. She had been told her dad had someone special in his life and that I was divorcing her dad. What her dad should have told her was that she was special in his life too. So again, Jesse was cheating on me and her. Lying in a marriage is one thing, but lying to a child who is his daughter is another. Jesse had been mysteriously missing, and I knew he was lying when he told me where he had been. You just know, don't you? Liars have a way of letting you know. Jesse had been telling Lexie that she would not see me again, and asking where she wanted to live.

As if Lexie had any choices here, in the sense of his actions, she was his target now. I took control on him and me when I chose to send that intense email back in April 2018.

I moved into the spare room; he never asked why. I remember one night going into the former martial bedroom where he was. He spoke, and so I sat on the bed. The next thing I remember is him on top of me giving it a sort of huff and puff, and he was finished, all over. I remember this distinctively because I could tell in that one night, he had used it elsewhere with another male or female. Not sure to this day what sex he wanted, hair pulling to the point it really hurt, grabbing, pinning you down or just the plain and simple, less than two minutes sex. Was I even the right sex for him? Looking at him in the courtroom it raises serious questions. Sometimes, it doesn't matter how many times you argue the facts; the evidence can be overwhelming. Even my gay friends were saying he was - so I was never sure.

I eventually got Lexie asleep in her bed, and I went into mine. I took the decision months ago to sleep in the spare room until I left. Lexie sobbed and sobbed; she knew what was happening around her. She said she hated living with him; she was using my friend's house to escape his behaviours. She didn't want to be near him. She hated me leaving her behind; in fact, I took her everywhere with me to ensure she was safe for at least a year or more. It became the only way to keep her safe; it sounds bonkers but truthful.

The next morning after being awake all night, as they say, I grabbed a pair of big-girl pants and put them on.

That morning I sought advice and guidance from the Women's Refuge local police and Social Services. They had always been telling me to leave when there was no storm. Getting up on this Friday was the one day where there was no storm, and Jesse was out of the house. After waiting three months and nineteen days, the time had come. There was no storm, no undercurrent. Jesse had stormed off to work; I awoke Lexie to ask her if she was ready to leave. She had cried herself to sleep; I could not get her out of bed for school. She just simply couldn't go on, I guess, nor could I. I was done too. I contacted her school to let them know we were going to run away from Jesse.

There was no discussion with Jesse- I just left at the right time for Lexie and me. I wrote three notes out, all saying the same thing: I was walking out on him as I was advised to do. I have one weekend where I think the dog suffered at his hands too. There was no way the dog was staying behind subjected to Jesse's behaviours. Our dog had to come with us, and a good job he has too. He's been a massive help to Lexie and me, kept us safe when we didn't feel it.

I eventually found the courage and strength to leave, as my saviour of a friend was right by my side. So armed with the child, Lexie's dog, car and two bags, we left him and our life. I went through a horrific incident-packed life that still, to this day, I cannot fully tell you what has happened to me, Lexie, or the dog. Some things have been left out as it's still too painful to say, read, or let you in on.

I am not a strong person; I did the exact right thing to escape – I believe he would have killed me for sure. I didn't split the family up, but if that one vile male could not accept responsibility for his actions, it was my time to take responsibility for Lexie and me. Without the Women's Refuge guidance, I bet I still would have been there being used as a battering ram.

My first task in the car was to obtain two new mobiles and phone numbers. What I also should have focused on was to have removed the tracker that was placed on my car without my knowledge or consent.

When you are brave enough to face the facts and incidences, take a deep breath and walk into a police station. The police will ask you one simple question to start with, which seems weird "Was your partner ever violent to an animal?"

You might choose to deny it, or you might find that courage to say yes, they were.

The police will respond, "You were living with a narcissist, domestic abuser, and you've done the right thing." At this point, you are starting on another road that there is no way of coming back from. Once you get to this moment, what could be any worse? It can be very lonely and testing, draining and exhausting, to say the least. But for me, deep down, I had to fight to escape every day and every hour. I started to lead a very different life.

So, let's have a small recap. I had my daughter, dog, car, new mobiles, legal representation, beautiful and supportive friends, Domestic Abuse teams and Women's Refuge behind me. What could possibly go wrong?

I think it's important to tell you that unless you have hospital documents to say you have had repeated incidences of violence against you, you stand very little chance of escaping. I can also warn you of the fact you will get one or two people doing the Flying Monkey process with you. A flying monkey is a relative or friend who is in your company 24/7 to solely record what you are up to and feed it back to your abuser. You will have been gaslit for the past however many years you have been with this person, so you will not know who to trust and what they say to you.

A narcissist will blame you for everything. Any of your actions can be manipulated to reflect how messed up they want you to think you are, which is what you learn in counselling.

You may have an older relative or friend who doesn't believe you have been domestically abused because you're not covered from head to toe in bruises. It may even be a professional too, which I experienced. Many people claimed that neither my child nor I witnessed or endured any domestic abuse. You won't have gathered all the evidence before you leave, but please don't worry; you're not calculating like your partner. You might even return to your partner on several occasions because you will still be able to be brainwashed into taking them back and forgiving them. You will also find that you can be led backwards as you're physically and mentally drained beyond any of your previous experiences within your life.

At that point, help starts to arrive. A hand from an unexpected place will guide you to a better path. Keep yourself protected and safe until help is in place.

I have been totally fortunate with six or seven amazing friends that have ensured Lexie and I are safe. These loyal, strong, and admirable friends are the reason my story is being exposed. They have stopped me from doing some serious, crazy stuff. Without them, I would be absolutely nothing. I am also blessed to play a part in a young woman's life and watch her develop. I hope she will remember what happened to her one day. But she's not ready to heal just yet. It's all got so very lost.

Lexie has trauma amnesia, eating disorder and self-harms mildly, but because she doesn't use a blade, she does not quantify for professional help. I know; I can hear you screaming "What?" The frustrations for you to navigate yourself through the system will test every single ounce of flesh from you. People do not have the knowledge or understanding. In my experience, if you're fleeing to gain space and move counties, you will experience differences in understanding domestic abuse and violence within police forces.

Family courts and the Cafcass process is horrific but well documented on good ole "Google." Assisting agencies within Family Courts are torn between whom to believe about what is going on. Despite one agency strongly recommending courses to assist the other parent, THEY will not do them, and there is no one to ensure that this happens. The silly thing is that that forces you to make choices you possibly wouldn't have considered.

I can share a powerful statement I have learnt from a great Domestic Abuse Specialist Counsellor - "play your games, not theirs." Anything you do or try will not change the person they are, so please preserve your energy for you and the child or children. You are, in this timeframe of leaving your home, silenced to have your say. However, once you break everything down into bite-sized issues, you will cope a little better.

One day, I will write about life since I left, including where I am today, and you will be amazed.

The start of a new chapter of life is nearby; now go for it. If I can write this, you can feel me on your shoulders wishing you strength and guiding you to where you want to be.

I have lost everything he has it all, it's been binned, thrown, stolen, sold, robbed and lied about, but I have gained something of a life for me and Lexie. Thirty-three years of working life with nothing to show for it. But for now, I have escaped with two especially important aspects of my life: my child and the dog.

I would love nothing more than anything to think I am free! But I'm not there yet after more than 48 months.

I am one of the thousands of women who have taken these hard steps to leave an abusive situation. But don't worry, as you might have guessed, there was already a female in the background who's taken my place way before I left - she even has my belongings and my life. Mind you there's been others involved in this sick relationship all along.

"Crack on love." At least I had the courage to raise the alarm bells. Not many do.

As I write the above, my web is a little looser, and I am learning to live without his web around me. I fight most days to keep my head above the parapet; I have had to be so patient and tolerate whilst absolutely everything has been thrown at me. I would like to think I have fought very hard, but now it's time for me to live, and so can you.

"Life within an abusive relationship starts with a heart and a diamond but sadly leaves you feeling like you need a club and a spade"

References of Help that Have Been Our Rocks to Survive

A hairdressing salon that took us under their wing – when we didn't have coats nor haircuts.

A small group of incredibly supportive friends.

An Estate Agent – Dina and her team.

Counsellors Helen and Myke.

Domestic Abuse Support specialists.

DRASACS.

Experian.

First Direct mortgage company.

Iceberg litigation loan.

Lincolnshire's foodbanks.

Lincolnshire's Refuge.

Lincolnshire's Social Services.

Lloyds Bank.

My landlord.

My legal team.

Nottinghamshire Education.

Nottinghamshire Social Services.

South Yorkshire foodbanks team, including Mo with her fresh, smiley face.

South Yorkshire Police Force.

South Yorkshire Social Services.

The loans from friends.

To two special people who gave us a TV and a TV licence.

To my special friend who sent shoebox deliveries that bought smiles to our faces.

To two special people who saw me walk into a damp-infested place and suddenly found us duvets, bedding, even a fruit bowl, in very dark hours.

Warwickshire Police Force.

Warwickshire Social Services.

Warwickshire's Refuge.

West Midlands Police.

Wider and Family Community Officers - Adult's Health and Wellbeing.

Women's Refuge Helpline.

Printed in Great Britain
by Amazon

83973914R00058